Reaching

BEYOND

EXCELLENCE

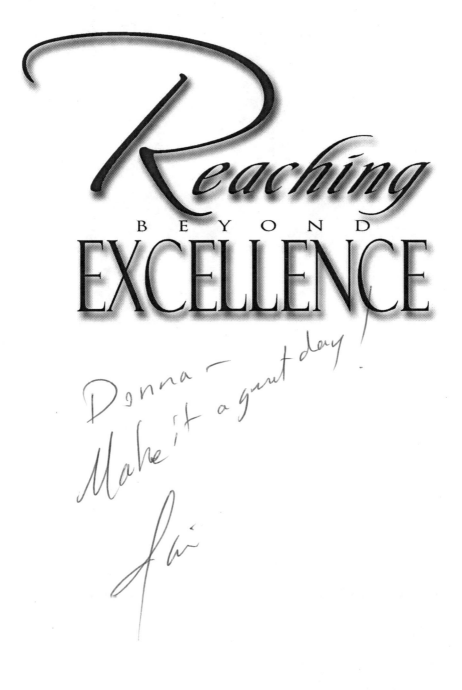

Donna —
Make it a great day!

Reaching

B E Y O N D

EXCELLENCE

PROVEN STRATEGIES
FOR *skyrocketing* PRODUCTIVITY
AND ENHANCING EVERYDAY LIFE

JIM MATHIS

Advantage™

Published by Advantage, Charleston, South Carolina.
Member of Advantage Media Group.

ADVANTAGE is a registered trademark and the
Advantage colophon is a trademark of Advantage Media Group, Inc.

Printed in the United States of America

ISBN: 978-1-59932-029-8

Most Advantage Media Group titles are available at special quantity discounts for bulk purchases for sales promotions, premiums, fundraising, and educational use. Special versions or book excerpts can also be created to fit specific needs.

For more information, please write: Special Markets, Advantage Media Group, P.O. Box 272, Charleston, SC 29402 or call 1.866.775.1696.

TABLE OF CONTENTS

PART I
PUTTING FIRST THINGS FIRST

chapter 1

LIVING WITH PURPOSE:
WHAT'S YOUR ONE THING?

"Above all be of single aim; have a legitimate and useful
purpose, and devote yourself unreservedly to it."
-James Allen

One of my favorite hobbies is watching old movies. I love getting lost in another time and place. It's not the escapism that appeals to me. The movies I like best are true stories. But the best fictional movies can have elements that feel true as life itself.

That's how one of my favorite movies, *City Slickers* (1991), feels to me. It's about a 39- year-old man who goes on a cattle drive with two friends to find his inner self.

For me, the central scene revolves around two characters, played by Jack Palance and Billy Crystal, when they're alone on the range, looking for a lost cow. Jack plays a crusty old cowboy with few emotions other than anger, as far as Billy can tell.

At one point, Jack says, cynically, "Yeah, you all come out here at about the same age. Same problems. Spend fifty weeks a year getting knots in your rope then -- then you think two weeks up here will untie them for you. None of you get it. Do you know what the secret of life is?"

Billy asks him.

"This!" Jack holds up one finger.

"Your finger?" asks Billy.

"One thing," Jack answers. "Just one thing. You stick to that and everything else don't mean anything."

"That's great, but what's the one thing?" Crystal asks.

"That's what you've got to figure out," Jack says.

These are not elegant words but they speak volumes to our day and age.

As Jack Handley once said, "I hope life wasn't a joke, because I didn't get it."

The question is, do *you* get it? What's your "one thing?" Have you figured it out yet?

To accomplish anything in life, you need to live invigorated by a compelling sense of purpose. But how can you live a life of purpose, when you don't know what your purpose is?

WHAT YOUR PURPOSE SHOULD LOOK LIKE

Jack didn't give Billy any hints. It didn't make it any easier. When you're looking for your "one thing," it helps a lot to know what you're looking for. Here are a few ways to recognize your purpose. You'll know it when you find it, because it should have the qualities I've mentioned below.

1. Your Purpose should start with you.
Your Talent.
What do you do well?

Everyone has a talent for something. Maybe you learned about your talent as a child, while you were performing for your classmates. Maybe your talent became a hobby in your teen years. Perhaps you developed a finesse for something that everyone else relies on you for today.

Your Desire.
What you want to do?

Is there something you have always wanted to do? Remember the 1981 movie *Chariots of Fire*, about the British Olympians in 1920? In that Oscar-winning film, Eric Liddell, the Christian Scottish runner, told his sister that the reason he enjoyed running was that he got great joy from it. He could feel God's power flowing through him when he ran. What do you do that makes you feel that passionate?

Your Results.
What do you accomplish when you're doing what you do well?

What abilities do you possess that help you do certain tasks better? You know what you are good at. My pastor often says that everyone is a 10 at something. What are you a 10 at?

Your Recognition.
What do others think you do well?

Ask your close friends or family what you "shine" at. What abilities do they see in you that you don't? Often others see abilities and gifts in us that we don't see ourselves. Your greatest supporters are the ones that see your strengths and can help you move toward them for success.

Your Circumstances.

What do you have the opportunity to do?

There is a verse in the Bible in the story of Esther. Her uncle tells her at a crossroads in her life, "Perhaps you have come into the kingdom for such a time as this." Where have you been placed at the right time to affect your own or others' destinies? What have you got at your disposal that no one else has, to solve problems or create a new way of doing things?

Your Fulfillment.

What do you enjoy doing?

What would you do, even if nobody paid you to do it? Remember, most people are a 10 at something. That thing, whatever it is, automatically gives them fulfillment and joy. If you can find out what this is in your life, find a way to get people to pay you and you've got it made! A friend once gave me some great advice, "Spend the first half of your life finding what you are best at doing and enjoy, and the second half getting people to pay you to do it."

2. **Your Purpose should contain life-changing convictions.**

Your convictions are the things for which you would lay down your life. Most people would agree that there are four things worth dying for:

(1) **Faith**

Our faith is what sustains us in tough times. Mel Gibson's movie, *The Passion of the Christ*, has caused many to discover (or rediscover) their faith. We all believe in something or someone. The first step in the 12-step Alcoholics Anonymous program is to acknowledge a Higher Power. Our faith is worth fighting and giving our lives for. Christians believe that Jesus laid down his life for the world. He said that there is no greater love than laying down your life for others.

(2) **Family**

Most good parents would easily lay down their lives for their children or each other. When you've got nothing else, you have your family. You may not have a great relationship with your parents or your siblings, but they are a source of support and strength when relationships are handled right.

(3) **Freedom**

Many Americans take this for granted. Statistics show that immigrants to our country are more successful in business than natural-born Americans. Why? Often they have fought hard to win their freedom and come to our shores and when they arrive, they keep fighting for their dream.

(4) **Friends**

You are doing very well in life, if you can name one or two close friends whom you trust and would lay down your life for (and who would do the same, in turn, for you). What have you done to cultivate close friendships with one or two people that will stand the test of time? An unknown author once said, "It is better to have lived for something than never to have lived at all."

3. Your Purpose should include others.

Don't have a goal for just yourself. Your Purpose should lift up and inspire everyone around you to a higher level. What are you doing that will change the lives of those around you?

John Maxwell says, "There is no success without a successor." You don't want people to say, after you hare dead and buried, "Thank goodness he/she is gone!" Leave this a better world than when you came. Bring others along with you.

Jimmy Durante, the famous comedian and entertainer of the Fifties, said, "Be awfully nice to them going up, because you're gonna meet them all coming down."

4. Your Purpose should be bigger than yourself.

Live for something greater than yourself. Your Purpose should be the last thing you accomplish. That way, your life is a continual effort to perfect your Purpose.

Ask yourself, "In 500 years (or in 50) will anyone know what I did? Will I have made a difference?" The really great contributions to mankind have lasting value that we all remember. Often the greatest inventions are created by people who want to make life better for everyone else. A friend of mine says he likes to give to worthy charities that truly do good for people because it not only helps them but makes him feel good, too.

5. Your Purpose should have eternal value.

Tom Winninger, a consultant to corporations, once met with the Board of Directors at an international film manufacturing corporation to show them how to beat their competition and become No. 1 in the market. They were concerned about another film making more sales than they were.

Tom surprised them by saying that the film corporation didn't sell film. The CEO argued that they did, but Tom insisted that they didn't.

After an exasperating conversation, the CEO said, "Well, before we dismiss you as our consultant, tell me what you think we do sell!"

Tom answered, "You sell memories. People don't buy film. They buy memories."

Tom gave these executives a vision. He showed them their product's eternal value. Every sale was more than just a roll of film; it was people's lives and dreams.

Your Purpose should be more than tangible, material things. It must include what matters to you most deeply, what has eternal value – for you and others.

As you search for your Purpose, ask yourself these questions: What are you a "10" at? Does that thing include others? Is it greater than yourself? Will it have a lasting impact?

Keep asking until you find the answers. Answering these questions will have a lasting impact on how you spend the rest of your life.

Chapter 2
GETTING YOUR PRIORITES RIGHT:
PUTTING YOUR PURPOSE FIRST

"The secret of success is the constancy of purpose."
~ Benjamin Disraeli

Whether they know it or not, people are failing today because they don't put their Purpose first. As a result, they lack the ability to set and keep priorities. In many cases, they have not taken the time to identify their Purpose. But, even when they know their Purpose, they fail to put it at the center of their lives and base their choices on that Purpose. They fail to make the main thing the main thing.

Life is about choices. You choose how you act and react to everyday situations. We choose the priorities we value. Our priorities trickle down to our daily routines.

When you ask people why they spend so much time doing things that aren't in keeping with their main Purpose, they always have many excuses. The excuses are so widespread that they've become very familiar.

The Seven Most Popular Excuses:

1. We do what we like to do before we do what we don't like to do.
2. We do things that provide the most immediate closure.
3. We do the quick tasks first.
4. We respond on the basis of who wants it.
5. We work on things in order of their arrival.
6. We work on the basis of the "Squeaky Wheel" principle.
7. We respond on the basis of the consequences for doing nor not doing something.

It's easy to tell ourselves these excuses aren't very important. If we do whatever comes in front of us and manage to stay busy all day, we can come home feeling like we've been productive. But have we lived under the guidance of our true Purpose? And, if we haven't, are we really making the best use of our time?

Whether or not we are willing to admit it or are even aware of it, the many distractions that occur during the day all involve priority decisions. Whenever we decide, for whatever reason, to engage in one action, we decided at that point against engaging in another.

It's important to remember, though, that finishing tasks is the goal, not the activity around them. We need to stay focused on achieving our goals so we won't fall into the trap of constantly changing priorities and staying busy just to be busy. This way, we can determine our priorities in terms of results, rather than activities.

"The fault lies within ourselves," Shakespeare wrote. We all tend to define our priorities in terms of activities.

Surveys reveal that, out of 100 people, 23 do not know what they want (leaving 77 who do know). Sixty-seven do know, but don't know how to get it (leaving 10 who know how). Of those 10 who know what they want and how to get it, 8 are unwilling to pay the price. Only 2 out of 100 will ever reach their goal because they set their priorities, have developed a plan and are willing to pay the price. Where do you fall in this list?

SETTING YOUR OWN PRIORITIES

Here are some imperatives for setting priorities to get you started on the path to achieving what you want in life.

When we set priorities, we need to now what we are here to accomplish -- whether in our jobs or our lives. When we set priorities, we need to have a good understanding of cause-and-effect relationships on our job.

It all comes back to finding our Purpose. We need to know not only what activities lead to accomplishing that Purpose, but how they rank in their importance toward reaching our goals.

The problem is that most of us decide when to do activities at work based on their importance or urgency, rather than on whether it matches our Purpose.

The reason this isn't effective is that *all activities* have some degree of importance. So it's easy for us to justify doing almost anything worthwhile!

FOUR TYPES OF ACTIVITIES

Activities generally fall into one of four categories. Let's look at these four to see how we can better determine what to do and when to achieve success and mastery over our time on the job.

1. **Important and Urgent.**

These are things are those that contribute significantly to our goals; they have high value. The relate directly to the organization's goals and meeting customer needs immediately. The more direct the contribution, the more important the activity. Important things also tend to have long-term consequences. They make a difference for a long time.

To find out your most important and urgent tasks, try the well-known *Paretto Principle*. Vilfredo Paretto was a 19th Century economist who came up with the 80/20 principle that can be applied to setting priorities.

List your top 10 priorities, then circle the first and second. Taking care of those two things will make the other 8 fall in line. Therefore, concentrating on the top 20% of your priorities will accomplish the remaining 80% involuntarily. In business it has been proven using this principle that 80 percent of profits may come from 20 percent of a business's customers. Try it for yourself. You'll be amazed at the results.

2. **Important, but not Urgent.**

These tasks are things you need to get done, but you can do them over a period of time. They should be scheduled second in importance, but have priority over everything else.

Like Important and Urgent things, they make a difference over a long time. They are in line with your general goals for the present and for the long term. Even though we know how important it is to prioritize our work, many of us still have difficulty focusing on the most important tasks at hand. It is sometimes tempting to get into "activity mode" and just keep working on clearing our desks, without focusing on doing the most important things first.

Again, Paretto helps us out with his discovery that only the top two goals are critical. If 80% of our activities will produce only about 20% of the results we want, then 20% will produce 80% of the results. We simply need to learn how to concentrate on the high-value important things (those which help us achieve our goals) and take care of those two items first.

3. **Urgent, but Not Important.**

These things account for most of the distractions we face each day at work. They have short-term consequences and must be done NOW! They won't wait. They may or may not relate to our goals or make a significant contribution to the world, but urgent things are for more demanding than important things. They involve telephone calls, memos, interruptions by often well-meaning individuals and emergencies. Often we set ourselves up, though to receive distractions by welcoming them. We have become our own worst enemy in handling our priorities.

To help you deal with these unplanned distractions, schedule your time and be ruthless about adhering to it. You will quickly find that most of the "urgent" distractions weren't that urgent and could wait.

Schedule a "quiet time" into your day when nothing is allowed to distract you. During this quiet time you will be accomplishing important tasks. Distractions can be put on hold unless they are of a nature that they MUST be given attention immediately – if the building is on fire, for instance! You will find distractions coming to you less frequently as people discover that you won't allow interruptions to get in the way of doing your job.

4.   Neither Important Nor Urgent.

These items are things we do in the course of the day that waste our time. Answering unimportant emails, returning telephone calls that aren't urgent and generally doing tasks that either can be put off or be delegated to someone else.

What are you doing that another associate with either more time or a better ability to accomplish mundane tasks could be doing? Often you will find that someone has been putting their mundane tasks off on you—until now.

Schedule one or two times a day when you will accomplish these tasks. Email is a constant. Most people don't expect an answer within 24 hours. Most people are surprised by a returned telephone call within 24 hours (or at all). The excuse, "I/We never get around to it" amounts to a white flag of surrender to unimportant and not urgent interruptions.

As your set your priorities in line with your Purpose, you will have less interruptions and more time to accomplish what you want to do. You will find yourself becoming more successful in life. You will find others re-orienting their schedules to accommodate yours out of respect for your "valued time." You will find more time to do what you want to do and less of what others expect you to do in their place.

What are you waiting for? *Begin today* to prioritize tomorrow's schedule. Demonstrate the wisdom, courage and discipline to do the important things first. Ask yourself:. What am I here to accomplish in life? What is my Purpose?

Once you know that, you can answer the smaller questions more easily: What jobs require me and me alone to accomplish them? What can someone else (who might have more time) do better? What must be done immediately? What tasks can I schedule at a more appropriate time? When will I schedule my "quiet time?" Try it out for several weeks and notice how your job suddenly becomes less hectic and your life starts to feel like it's finally on track.

Chapter 3

CHANGES IN ATTITUDES, CHANGES IN ALTITUDES:
HOW YOUR ATTITUDE CAN IMPROVE THE QUALITY OF YOUR LIFE

"People only see what they are prepared to see"
~ *Ralph Waldo Emerson*

*D*id you know that if you take the letters in the word "ATTITUDE" and assign them their numerical order in the English alphabet (A=1, T=20, T=20, I=9, T=20, U=21, D=4 and E=5), it adds up to 100. Attitude is 100%! "Success" only adds up to 93.

When you realize that your attitude is the key to success, you have most of the battle won. So are you ready to take a journey into improving your level of living by improving your attitude?

FIVE TRUTHS ABOUT YOUR **ATTITUDE**

Once you learn these five truths about your attitude, you will be more successful than you have ever dreamed!

1. You choose your attitude.
The story of Jim Stovall is a perfect illustration of this first truth.

Jim was a very good high school football player in Oklahoma. His dream was to play football for the Oklahoma University Sooners. But during a routine physical at age 17, he was told that he was progressively losing his sight. By 19, he was legally blind. His athletic dreams dashed, he sat home in front of his television and listened to old movies. He tried several jobs assisting handicapped children, but wasn't truly happy.

Then one day in his early twenties, while Jim was listening to old movies, he got the idea that he might narrate the movies so blind people could tell what was happening on the screen. Jim was very excited, but almost everyone he spoke to told him that his idea was ridiculous. At every turn he was met with discouragement, but Jim believed in his idea. Undaunted by the opposition, he just worked harder.

First, he started narrating a local television show in Tulsa and interviewed any producer, director or star as they passed through town. He produced narrations for the movies in his own basement. After several trips to New York (and more discouraging comments), he formed what is now known as the Narrative Television Network.

Today Jim is a famous speaker and Network executive. His advice: When people tell you that your idea won't work, ignore them and they'll go bother someone else. Attitude is a choice.

2. You get what you expect out of life.

Psychology 101 teaches you this. One of my favorite "philosophers," Flip Wilson, said it better: "What you see is what you get."

Several years ago, I tried out this truth with my daughter, when she was on her way to Girl Scout Camp. She had a bad day on Monday on her way to camp. On Tuesday, I told her she would have the day she expected and urged her to say, "It's going to be a great day!" I suggested she repeat this mantra before every activity. When it was time for crafts, she would say, "It's going to be a great day." When her group went swimming, she would say, "It's going to be a great day." She agreed to try it out and see what happened.

That afternoon when I picked her up, she said, "I've had a wonderful time at camp today. Daddy, you were right. It *was* great day!" Like all of us, she had exactly the day she expected.

3. Your attitude determines your relationship with other people.

In a Stanford Research Institute study, it was found that most job successes were 87% people knowledge and only 13% product knowledge. It doesn't matter what you know, it's who you know and how you treat them.

Earl Nightingale once said, "People don't care how much you know until they know how much you care." You get back the attitude you send out to other people.

Have you ever shown up for work feeling great and someone asked you why you were in such a bad mood? One person can't usually talk you into being angry, but if two or three people start asking you what is wrong, before you know it your really ARE in a bad mood! How does that happen? You let other people determine your attitude.

Have you ever had a "bad hair day?" Did you notice how your attitude influenced everyone around you? Don't blame it on your hair, blame it on your attitude.

When it comes to your relationships with others, treat each person as if they are the most important person in the world and notice how it will change their attitude. You'll also notice that you will feel even better in return. You get back what you send out -- in abundance.

4. Your attitude will influence how you view problems.

How do you view problems now? Do you view them as set-backs or opportunities?

I once talked with a trucking COO who told me that he thought problems were just that --problems. He said, "When you've got a truck broken down on the side of the road somewhere, that's a problem."

What a negative view he had! What if you were that trucker beside the road waiting to be rescued? Wouldn't you want your supervisor to see your circumstance to be seen as an opportunity to help you? Wouldn't you as a supervisor want to send the message to other employees that when someone is in trouble in your firm, you will be quick to help them?

We can all learn from our problems. Problems can be like the warning lights on the instrument panel of your car. Did you know that every miracle in the Bible started with a problem? Isn't it nice to know that, if you have a problem, it automatically makes you a candidate for a miracle? If you don't have a problem, you don't get a miracle. Learn to look at problems as attitude enhancers, not destroyers.

5. Your attitude will raise your altitude in life.

My dentist has one of the most positive attitudes of anyone I've ever seen. His staff considers it a joy to work with and for him.

Several years ago, they wanted to take off more time at Christmas. So they could continue to log in enough hours to take off a couple of weeks at the end of December, they agreed to work on Fridays in autumn-- a day they were usually closed throughout the year.

So every Friday in autumn, when you come into their office for an appointment, you hear Christmas music being played over the intercom. The office is decorated for the Yuletide season – but only on Fridays! It's a way of keeping the goal in front of everyone. They not only stay focused on working to take off the two weeks at Christmas, but they have fun in the process.

Both the dental patients and his staff enjoy visiting the office from August through November on Fridays. And don't think it doesn't influence everyone's attitude the rest of the week. You might even say it "bleeds over." (A little dental humor...)

What is your attitude doing to help or hinder your level in life? Is it lifting you (and others) up or holding you down? Remember, it is your choice. No one gives you your attitude. The choice is yours.

PROFILES

JOHN MCCAIN

United States Senator John McCain (R-Arizona) has a very colorful past. His is a story of courage in the face of disaster, torture and continuing physical pain. It is a story worth telling.

Born August 29, 1936 in the Panama Canal zone, he was a third-generation naval officer. Both his father and his grandfather were well-known, four-star admirals in the United States Navy. They had both served their country in war time and John wanted to follow in their footsteps. At the age of 17, he chose to apply for entrance to the U.S. Naval Academy. After graduating from the Naval Academy, John trained to fly jets. He served for twenty-two years as an aviator.

While serving on the U.S. Forrestal Aircraft Carrier during his tour of duty in Vietnam, a disaster struck. John was in his plane on the flight deck when an errant missile from another aircraft fired and struck his fuel tanks. John 's plane burst into flames. He managed to get out of the plane by crawling over the nose. He could have escaped, but he turned back to help a fellow flyer. Before John could reach the burning man, more bombs exploded on the flight deck, blowing him back 10 feet. John received severe injuries in the incident.

It took a full day to contain the flames in the Navy's worst non-combat related disaster. Many men were killed and injured. When it was over, John could have gone home, but he volunteered to remain and was assigned to the U.S. Orinasky. It was a decision that would change his life forever.

Perhaps his greatest test came just three months after the Forrestal disaster in 1967. He was going on his twenty-third bombing run over Hanoi when he was shot down. He managed to press the ejection button in time, but the force of the ejection broke both of his arms and one of his legs.

Once he hit the ground in an injured state, an angry mob beat and kicked him, breaking his shoulder. As he tried to get away from them, the mob bayoneted him repeatedly. Yet somehow, he survived.

John McCain became one of the most well-known prisoners housed in the infamous "Hanoi Hilton." He was denied medical treatment for days after his capture and many of his fellow prisoners thought he was near death. As they cared for him, he slowly recovered.

Torture and starvation became commonplace to his life. For two years, he was suspended so often in solitary confinement that, to this day, he cannot lift his arms fully over his head. When his father, Admiral Jack McCain was appointed commander of all U.S. forces in the Pacific, the Vietnamese offered to early release John as a propaganda ploy. But as much as he was suffering, John refused, citing the Code of Prisoners of War, which states that prisoners must be released in order of capture. He refused early release so many times, that he drew the attention of his captors and they increased his torture and beatings.

Ultimately, he endured this suffering for over five-and-a-half years from 1967-1973. The world watched as he walked off the airplane in 1973 with the other returning Prisoners of War from the Vietnam War. His heroism inspired the country. Once he was home, John worked hard in rehabilitation to be cleared to fly for the Navy again.

Unfortunately, as with many returning POW's, his marriage ended several years later. Then, in 1980, he met and fell in love with Cindy Hensley in Phoenix and the two were married.

He was awarded the Silver Star, Bronze Star, Legion of Merit, Purple Heart and Distinguished Flying Cross. He retired as a captain in 1981. His last service for the Navy was liaison to the U.S. Senate. That is where John acquired the desire to serve his country in a new way.

In 1982, he ran for U.S. Representative from Arizona. John worked tirelessly to get elected. He campaigned door-to-door and outworked his five opponents to win the Republican primary and later the U.S. House seat in Congress. McCain came home every weekend to live in his community and worked so well as a public servant that he was re-elected two years later. When the legendary Arizona Senator Barry Goldwater announced his retirement in 1986, John sought and won his Senate seat. He ran for the Presidency in 2000 and continues to serve in the U.S. Senate today.

John McCain tells what he has learned about life and his upbringing in a famous naval family in his autobiography, **Faith of My Fathers**, which spent 24 weeks on the *New York Times* bestsellers list. In 1997, he was named one of the "25 Most Influential People in America" by *Time* magazine.

TOM BROKAW

On December 1, 2004, Tom Brokaw went out a winner. He retired from the news anchor chair of *NBC Nightly News*. He looks like the All-American success story and he is. But did you know that he struggled to achieve what he did? Life didn't just hand him the breaks. It never does.

Persistence and tenacity led Tom to the pinnacle of the field in his industry. Just like Fred Astaire, who was told he couldn't act and didn't dance well, and both Louisa May Alcott and Erma Bombeck, who were told they should give up writing, Tom faced rejection early in his career. Discouragement came to him when someone who was asked to serve as a reference for him wrote, "He can't type, is slow to work and, frankly, we're disappointed with his output." But Tom was determined to make it in his chosen field.

Tom Brokaw was born February 6, 1940, in Webster, South Dakota. Raised in a poor family, along with two brothers, Tom was interested in broadcasting in high school. Ultimately, he studied political science at the University of South Dakota.

While working at a radio station as a student, Brokaw professed his love on the air to his high-school sweetheart, Miss South Dakota. They were married after graduation and had four daughters. After college, Tom moved from radio to television stations in Omaha, Nebraska, where he worked for a salary of $100 salary, then he moved on to Atlanta, Georgia. He once said, "TV is a fickle business. I'm only good for the length of my contract.

Tom joined NBC working as a correspondent in California in 1966 and became a White House correspondent in 1973 at the height of the Watergate scandal. In an early foreshadowing of competition with another anchor, Tom was pursued by CBS to join their staff and replace Dan Rather at the White House, but when word leaked to the press the deal fell through. In 1976 Brokaw became anchor of the Today on NBC news and gained a national reputation for an optimistic and easygoing delivery of the news.

When John Chancellor retired in 1981 Tom co-anchored the *NBC Nightly News* with Roger Mudd, until he was chosen in 1983 to be the sole anchor for the prestigious position. Tom's fame was just beginning. In 1987 he held the first one-on-one American TV interview with Mikhail Gorbachev and won an A.I.duPont-Columbia University Award. That same year he scored an interview with President Ronald Reagan in the White House. He also moderated the debates among all declared presidential candidates of both parties the next year. Brokaw was reportedly the inspiration for William Hurt's Tom Grunick, the character in James L. Brooks' 1987 film *Broadcast News*.

Brokaw has been one of the most well-recognized participants in the trend toward expanding the role of the news reader into a prominent position of creative control and celebrity. He wasn't afraid of leaving the comfort of his anchor chair. He reported form the Berlin Wall in 1989, when it came down. In fact, he was the only on-air, American news anchor to personally witness the wall's collapse. He has interviewed the Dalai Lama and reported on Human Rights abuses in Tibet. He took the *NBC Nightly News* on the road to Beirut, Kuwait during the Gulf War, then to Somalia and Kosovo during the Balkan conflict. Adding to his *Nightly News* responsibilities, he hosted several news magazines, for which he earned many prestigious broadcasting awards.

To add to the numerous articles he has written for publications like *The New York Times*, *The Washington Post*, *Newsweek*, and *Life*, Brokaw became a bestselling author in 1998 with the release of his second book, **The Greatest Generation**, dedicated to the Americans who were raised during the Great Depression, fought in WWII and built the infrastructure for the America of today. After the success of the first book, Tom decided to publish a follow-up in 1999, entitled **The Greatest Generation Speaks.**

Tom left his anchor chair having crafted it into a new model for television news. Brokaw he has also shared his wealth, volunteering for Habitat for Humanity and donating $250,000 toward a hiking and biking trail in Yankton, South Dakota, his former hometown. An avid outdoorsman, he says he doesn't consider himself a star, just a regular guy that a lot of people happen to recognize as the face of *NBC News* for the past 20 years. It is that relaxed image that has helped make NBC the ratings winner among evening news watchers during his tenure. He has shown spirited determination in going for his life-long goal and putting first things first. His life is an inspiration.

PART II
Increasing Your Productivity

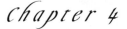

Chapter 4

BE CREATIVE:
10 BLENDS TO GET YOUR JUICES FLOWING

"Most people die before they are fully born. Creativeness
means to be born before one dies."
~Erich Fromm

The one question that I am asked most at conferences is this:

HOW CAN I BE MORE CREATIVE?

Creative people seem to have more fun in life. It's obvious to everyone, so people want to know how they can be more creative too. Creative people are indispensable to the executives and often climb very quickly up the ladder of life. So it makes sense for people to ask: What can we do to be more creative? What steps can we take to get the creative juices flowing?

I like to think of myself as a creative person. When I came up with "The Seven Dwarfs of Change" speech about coping with Change and Transition, I wanted people to remember the seven reactions to change in the opening exercise, so I searched my memory for something that came in sevens. Bang! It hit me: The familiar story of Snow White and The Seven Dwarfs. I've since gone on to other speeches, but this one gave me inspiration in the way it furthered my creative process.

That moment of inspiration is a good example of what being creative is to me: Looking for ways to make other things work better together. All of us are creative at some level. It's how our minds work. We're constantly looking for ways to make things work better together.

It's like mixing juices at a juice bar. Some work well together and others don't. But with a little creative ingenuity, you can sometimes hit on mixes that are truly inspired!

If you're wondering what you can do to enhance your creativity, however, here are 10 ways to do it. I like to think of them as 10 blends to get your creative juices flowing.

10 WAYS TO ENHANCE YOUR CREATIVITY

1. Network with creative people.

I get my best ideas at conferences and seminars where great speakers and "idea people" tell me what they are doing and how they came up with it. I especially love going to our National Speaker's association conventions, conferences and meetings.

Some of my best ideas come from hanging around these people who are the most creative people I know. We share ideas and challenge each other to go one step further. I belong to several organizations that involve entrepreneurs and creative people. Most are inexpensive and the ideas flow freely. Start going to events like these, if you can. Surround yourself with creative people and your own creativity will soar.

2. Look for/Do the obvious.

When I developed my speech on dealing with storms in life, I tried to find a way to get people interested from the outset by reminding them of something they were familiar with.

When I was a boy growing up, the only people I knew about who had been involved in a storm were the TV castaways on *Gilligan's Island*. Just about everyone from that era watched the TV show and knew who the characters were because the theme song told about each one of them. So I used *Gilligan's Island* in the introduction to my speech about how to survive terrible events in life, called "Trying to Reason with Hurricane Season."

Sometimes an obvious connection is the best connection. It gives you something in common with other people and sends out a creative spark to everyone.

3. Stay in search mode.

Look for many options continually. Albert Einstein has been credited with saying, "Doing the same thing over and over, expecting different results is the definition of crazy."

French philosopher Emile Chartier said, "Nothing is more dangerous than an idea when it's the only one you have." Always keep your eyes open for new ideas and options for age-old routines.

Robert Kreigel and Louis Patler wrote a great book on this subject, called, *If It Ain't Broke, Break It!*

When you're searching for creative ways to do things, remember that most good things come to an end. People who generate alternatives will have something to fall back on when the present solution is no longer effective. Stay involved in the creative process.

4. Look for solutions -- not faults.

We are constantly surrounded by fault finders. The creative person who not only can see what's wrong but provides a solution will get rewarded with more and better responsibilities.

Once again, Henry Ford said, "Don't find fault ... find a remedy."

Charles Kettering, when he was the head of General Motors, always told people to leave their slide rules behind when attending meetings, because participants would take them out and use them to compute fault with new ideas. We've moved from slide rules to calculators and laptops today, but the same principle still applies.

Try this: Don't discuss a problem unless you can provide some workable solution.

5. Be unreasonable.

Go for the un-reasoned response to problems and difficulties. Think differently.

Creative people don't waste time calculating. They think ahead, regardless of the consequences. Life is full of people who will refine or shoot down your ideas. Let them do it. Don't argue with them or try to win them over. Let it be a waste of their energy, not yours.

Spend your own time thinking outside of the box. And if that doesn't work, build your own box.

6. Always be thinking.

Practice mental calisthenics.

History records that Cyrus McCormick is not only known for inventing the reaper, but when his customers couldn't afford to buy his brilliant idea -- he invented installment plans to help farmers pay for it! Now *that's* creative thinking.

Develop a system to file your ideas so when the BIG one comes, you can make it mesh with several others.

If you don't file well, this is a great way to get a system started. Remember my *Gilligan's Island* idea for my "Trying to Reason with Hurricane Season" speech?

Right after that idea came to me, I saw an episode of the popular CBS series *Survivor*. *Gilligan's Island* also premiered on CBS back in the Sixties. In a way, it was the very first survivor series on CBS. (Except Gilligan didn't vote people off the island.)

In my talk on life's storms, that's one of the first things we do. We vote one of the seven castaways off *Gilligan's Island* -- just for the fun of it!

7. Get out of the Cookie Cutter mold.

Find ways to do things differently. Dare to be different. Don't bother with the criticism you receive.

Albert Einstein said, "Great spirits have *always* encountered violent opposition form mediocre minds." Learn to see what others refuse to see.

Go out and rent -- no, BUY -- the movie, *Patch Adams*, starring Robin Williams. It's the true story of a medical school student who challenges the norm and does medicine in creative ways. He is advised by a friend to see the world anew each day. When he does, he changes the lives of many people. You can, too!

8. See problems as opportunities.

John Maxwell says, "When we see problems as problems, we want to be controlling. But when we see problems as opportunities, we want to be creative." Seeing problems as opportunities is an important step toward living as a more creative person.

There is a famous story about a shoe company that sent a salesman to a South Seas island. After he arrived, the salesman wrote the company a desperate letter: "This place is a nightmare! Everyone is used to being barefooted and nobody wears shoes here. Send me home!"

The company recalled him and sent a second salesperson. This salesman wrote the company too:

"This place is paradise! Everyone here is a potential customer. Send more shoes!" Which salesman would you be? Do you see problems as overwhelming or do you see problems as opportunities?

9. Challenge rules and assumptions.

This is very difficult for personality/behavior types that feel they always have to abide by the rules.

History shows us that the most creative people were rules breakers. Thomas Edison hated playing by the rules. He believed that rules stifled creativity. One of his famous quotes about his workshop in Menlo Park, NJ was: "There ain't no rules around here. We're trying to accomplish something!"

The rules you are using to govern your life are often exactly the things that are keeping you from growing and being creative.

One of the most frequent complaints I hear in talking to executives is that their people don't use creative ways to cross-sell or extend themselves with customers. Then I find out that the workers are afraid to step out of the rules and try new ideas.

What are the rules governing your life? What do you do because you think you "ought to," even though it is stifling your creativity?

Identify these rules in your life, then deliberately challenge them. Experiment with more creative ways of living in your day-to-day life. You'll soon reap the rewards of creative living!

10. Have fun!

It's okay to enjoy your work and your life. In a recent survey it was revealed that an adult of 40 is about 2% as creative as a child of 5 years of age. The sad truth is that, by age 40, 98% of the creativity has been squeezed out of most of us.

Theodore Geisel (aka, Dr. Seuss) said, "Adults are obsolete children." Do you feel that your creativity has become obsolete?

A chart I saw one time said that ages 1-7 are filled with asking "Why?" By ages 7-17, they are filled with asking the question, "Why not?" But by the time they reach 17-70, they've stopped asking and are filled with a closed-door statement: "Because!"

If you want to be more creative, become a kid again. Start asking, "Why not?"

Creativity is the quality that can make you shine. It can turn your "bland" days into "blast-off" days. Whether you are living in a creative way or your creativity has become obsolete depends entirely on your attitude toward your circumstances and finding solutions.

When you live life as a creative person, your productivity is increased many times over because you are constantly coming up with new ideas and never letting problems get in your way. The creative life is not just a more enjoyable life, it's also the best way to get things done!

You make the choice. You can be creative, swimming upstream, keeping all your questions about life open to possibility --or you can just go with the flow, never engaging life or having fun. Which choice are you going to make? It's up to you.

Chapter 5

CHANGING HABITS TO MASTER YOUR TIME:
CHANGE BAD HABITS IN 21 DAYS (OR LESS!)

"First we make our habits, then our habits make us."
~John Dryden

"*Busy*" is the enemy of a life driven by Purpose. The key to having a more purposeful and productive life is to master your time, not increase your activities.

As the old saying goes, "Work smarter, not harder!"

For all of us, there are external forces constantly encroaching on our lives to distract us from fulfilling our true Purpose in life. You do not have to be at the mercy of these forces, even though it feels like it sometimes.

Take control of your thoughts and your time. The more you believe you *can* control, the more you will *try* to control, and the more you *will* control. It is entirely up to you.

Know this: You *can* master your time and take control of your life. After all, you can't change your past, but you can always change your future. Your time is your life. And as you master your time, you create a better life for yourself.

Apply your creativity to the problem. If you allow yourself to stay stuck in the old ways of doing things, you will never hit on the exciting new solutions that help you move from one success to the next. There is another old saying that makes an important point: "The more you do of what you're doing, the more you will get of what you've got."

Here are some tips to get you started on changing those old habits for good. Once you've put these to work in your life, use your own creative juices to start thinking of more! When you are living a Purpose-driven life, you focus on constantly growth as you move toward your goal.

Desire is the key to success or failure in changing any behavior. In order to change old work habits, you have to *want* to change. When you identify your Purpose in life, you quite naturally select something that you want more than anything else. Your desire to fulfill your Purpose is heightened. It's the ideal state for changing bad habits along the way.

Old habits can be hard to break, but many time-management experts tell us that in three to twenty-one days, most people can change their habits. If you consistently practice the new time-management behavior for three weeks, it will become the predominant response behavior. At that point, you will have replaced the old habit with the new one. But where do you start to replace self-defeating habits with self-reinforcing ones?

HOW TO DEFEAT YOUR BAD HABITS

1. Identify the Bad Habits.

To get things on track, so you are constantly moving toward your true Purpose, you must take control of your life. Old habits that have consistently interfered with your progress or kept you from your goals have got to go.

Begin by identifying the bad habits you want to change.

The more you know about what you do, when you do it and why, the easier it will be to identify habits that are hurtful or detrimental to your work life. This means you need to analyze your behaviors and the situations where they occur. Then identify the precise behaviors you want to change.

Examine your assumptions to see if any of them are holding you back from achieving the change you desire. Are consistently late for work or meeting deadlines? Examine the behaviors that lead to your not being on time. Maybe you like to stay up late and don't get up in time to get ready. Perhaps you allow outside (external) forces to control your time, causing you to not meet deadlines.

Often our worst habits have been with us for many years. If need be, look back over your early years for clues to your behavior. What were your study habits like in school? Did you have difficulty turning in assignments or starting them on time? The more you know about them, the better you'll be able change your old habits.

2. Create a New Habit.

One of the best ways to get rid of an old habit is to replace it with a new one. Don't leave a void where the old habit used to be. Replace it with something better. If you are in the habit of wasting your time on a Friday night, find something valuable to do instead. Make that your new habit.

Define the new habit you wish to develop. You might admire someone else who has mastered this habit and want to consult with them about how they developed this behavior. They might possess a habit you have been wanting to adopt for some time, but you have been putting the change off.

Now is the time to act! Procrastination is never your friend.

Begin by recording what you want to change on paper in a journal. Journaling is a great way to keep track of not only your time, but your progress as well. The best time masters keep track of their schedules, plans and goals, so they can keep tabs on their own progress to see where they have come from, and where they are going.

Learn to keep track of your time in a Day-Timer, Outlook or ACT Calendar, Personal Data Assistant (PDA) or similar method for recording your steps. You will improve your time-management habits only if you are honest with yourself and develop a realistic, doable action plan. Before you know it, a host of new, positive, life-affirming habits will fill your schedule, in place of the old bad habits you never wrote down!

3. Act with Purpose

Begin the new behavior as purposefully as possible. As the old saying goes, every journey starts with the first step. Make yours a step in the right direction.

Once you have identified the new habit you want to develop, tell people about it. If everyone knows what you're doing, you'll be less tempted to fall back into your old behavior.

Establish new routines associated with your new habit. Put up signs on your workstation, in your car or your bathroom mirror to remind you of your new behavior. It is important that you do everything possible to alter your environment to give the new habit a fertile place to take root and grow.

Listen to motivational tapes that both encourage and inspire you to change and stay with it. Associate songs or poems with the new habit that you can repeat to yourself or remember in your head as you stay with the new behavior.

It is also very important to set a date that you are aiming for you to have the new habit established as your regular behavior. Write it down. Establish a deadline. Remember: people who don't set goals rarely ever attain them.

4. Don't Give Up!

Never deviate until your new habit is firmly established. Keep the pressure on!

My friend and fellow speaker, Joe Bonura, tells of a young man who was working on a marketing campaign. He had some successes and failures. Curiously enough, the successes did more harm than the failures.

Once he succeeded, he decided he didn't have to work as hard the next day. Sure enough, each day thereafter, he worked less and less on his plan. After just one week, he had lost his rhythm and motivation for his marketing campaign. A new habit has to be consistently reinforced with positive behavior. Eliminate the phrase, "Just this once won't matter" from your vocabulary. It will matter.

In my keynote speech, "The Seven Dwarfs of Change," I used to talk about Sneezy. Remember Sneezy? He would sneeze constantly, but when a finger would be put under his nose, the convulsions would cease. The minute, though the finger was removed ... KA-BOOM! He'd sneeze stronger than before.

When you're trying to establish a new habit, think of yourself as Sneezy. Don't let take the pressure off or you'll explode back onto your old habits worse than ever.

5. Get Help

Ask other people to help you change. Find someone to hold you accountable. Rarely do we make significant changes in our behavior without the support of others. Family, friends and co-workers are usually great sources of support because they typically have a vested interest in your welfare.

Think carefully about who might be able to help you. Ask yourself who has supported you in the past and who truly believes in you. Go to the person (or people) who always think you can do it. Seek out those in whom you have trust and in whose advice you place value. Choose members of your support team wisely. How could they help you best? What responsibilities will you put on them to help you out? If you build a strong support team around you, new habits are much easier to master.

6. Reap the Rewards

Reward yourself for attaining your goal of adopting a new habit. Don't think of it as self-indulgence. It's an important part of change. What gets rewarded gets done. It's that simple.

Find some luxury or special treat that you value highly to reward yourself when you know you have completed your change of habit. It might be a meal out at your favorite restaurant, a movie you treat yourself to, or a trip to a place that is enticing enough to help you stay with your plan to change that old habit. Make a reservation in advance, if that helps you stay focused, but don't treat yourself until you have truly made the new behavior a habit.

Then, go all out and celebrate with your support team. Bring those along who helped you get there. It will make the party that much richer and more memorable for you.

As rewarding as it can be to eliminate bad habits and create new ones for yourself, the best part is what comes next. Once you've learned how to do it, you can encourage others (just as others helped you) to change their behavior for the better. Take what they did for you and pass it forward. "And," as the song says, "the world will be a better place..."

Chapter 6

THINKING YOUR WAY TO THE TOP:
WHERE ARE YOU CHOOSING TO BE?

"1500 years ago, everybody knew that the Earth was the center of
the Universe; 500 years ago everybody knew that the world was flat:
and five minutes ago you thought we were alone on this planet.
Imagine what you'll know tomorrow."
-Tommy Lee Jones, Men in Black (1997)

*R*ecently, I have read a stack of books and articles on improving your attitude through improving your mind. One of the best is *Success through a Positive Mental Attitude*, by Hill and Stone. As a result, I am continually improving the way I look at people and events and raising my level of living.

It is possible to continue to educate yourself beyond what government or private schools will do for you. Although he lived on the American frontier, Abraham Lincoln read voraciously. He became a self-made scholar. He carried a positive attitude with him in life. It helped him overcome a string of election losses before he won the presidency of the United States twice -- against seemingly insurmountable odds.

The simple fact is: You are where you are because that is where you've chosen to be, for one reason or another.

What are you doing to advance your life on a day-to-day basis? What are you doing to improve the world you live in and the lives of those around you daily? What factors can you control in your thinking to elevate your standard of living? Chris Hodges says, "The way we think often sets our destiny."

FIVE WAYS TO MAKE DECISIONS

Here are five ways to make decisions that will start you thinking your way to success:

1. Question popular thinking.

Popular thought is usually wrong. It follows trends and fads without any base in the real world. Learn to tell fads from reality. In 2005, it seemed that everyone was enthralled with Dan Brown's book, *The DaVinci Code*. Although it is a work of fiction, the story of the book has found its way into popular thinking. People are changing their entire belief systems based on a fictional book that has created a "buzz."

Don't let the "buzz" sting you. Fad/trendy topics and thinking come and go. Learn to base your attitude and vision on tried-and-true reality. The book of Ecclesiastes in the Bible says, "There is nothing new under the sun."

It is unlikely that some new get-rich-quick scheme or magical path to prosperity is going to succeed more readily than the principles you've always known, but have never gotten around to applying in your life. It is also unlikely that the constant forecasts of doom-and-gloom are going to come true in your lifetime.

My advice? Get a life. A real one, not one based on the latest trend.

2. Unleash the potential of focused thinking.

Imagine the possibilities if you could learn to concentrate on solving your top two problems in life in order to achieve all the others.

What if you could give your full attention to your greatest needs or your wildest dreams? The results would be phenomenal. Yet most of us don't organize our time, so we are at the mercy of every interruption. It is increasingly hard to stay focused on your dreams and goals.

Take your thoughts captive! Make them obedient to your vision. Practice the art of focusing your thoughts on success for one week and watch the improvement in your life.

My advice: Imagine the possibilities.

3. Unlock the power of possibility thinking.

What is your greatest dream? What would you do if you truly believed you were invincible? Why are you limiting yourself in your thinking? Start using your imagination to see what you can achieve. Do you ever let yourself ask, "What might be?" or "What if...?"

Your world is no bigger than your brain. Enlarge your mind and enlarge your world of possibilities. You can transform yourself by renewing your mind.

The best way to start is to eliminate the word "impossible" from your vocabulary. People who see themselves as failures use this word too often in their conversations both with others and themselves.

My advice: Never say "impossible" again

4. Embrace the lessons of reflective thinking.

Make it a habit to recall the victories you have experienced in the past. Many people today say you should ignore your past and only look to the future. The trouble with that is that it will cause us to forget what we have accomplished! How will you know what successes you can build on in the future, if you never remember what you've achieved in the past?

Begin keeping a journal to document the feelings and desires you have today. It will be interesting to look back on it in three, six and twelve months from now to see where you were and how far you have come.

Find a time each day to quietly contemplate your vision and goals. Allow no interruptions during this Quiet Time. Ruthlessly guard it. After three weeks it will become a habit if you stick to it and it will become a time that you look forward to each day.

My advice: Confidence can be found in past successes.

5. Experience the joy of unselfish thinking.

Remember, when you are down and depressed, life is not about you. Life is bigger than that.

Usually when we worry about what people are thinking, those people aren't really thinking about us at all! They're caught up in their own lives. Hard as it may be to believe, we are not the center of the universe for other people. When you let this truth sink it, it's actually a relief. You'll be well on your way to experiencing the joy of unselfish thinking.

Learn to give of yourself and your prosperity. Kahlil Gibran said, "You give but little when you give of your possessions. It is when you give of yourself that you truly give." The Dead Sea is "dead" because it continually receives and never gives.

Few people can name three major lottery winners, but most people can name great philanthropists, like: Stanford, Duke, Stetson, LeTourneau and Newman (Paul Newman gives proceeds from his sales of condiments and dressings to charities every year).

Henry Ford once said, "You won't be remembered for what you received in life, but for what you gave away to others." Try to leave this world a better place when you depart it than when you entered. What ideas can you use to benefit others? What are you involved in that is bigger than yourself? Are you leaving a YOU-shaped hole in the world that will be hard to fill when you are gone?

My advice: Decide it's not all about you.

FIVE WAYS TO THINK YOUR WAY TO THE TOP

What does it take to make the decisions and organize your thoughts into a real plan to make your life better? Earl Nightingale said, "You become what you think about." He was absolutely right. Here are five ways you can change your thinking to create the best kind of success in your life.

1. **Find a Strategic Plan to control your thoughts.**
   The best way to defeat a thought is to replace it with a higher thought. Constantly strive to find better ideas and higher thoughts.

   Ask yourself how you are working toward achieving your Purpose. Most people have no idea what they want in life. If you are determined to live your Purpose the odds are stacked in your favor.

   Why? Less than a third of the population has written their Purpose down. Ten percent of all people know how to get there, but only two will ever try.

   Hill and Stone in *Success Through a Positive Mental Attitude* say that if you control your thoughts, you will succeed in life. Your thoughts direct your path.

   "As a man thinks, so he is." says the famous proverb. You are what you believe you are. Believe in yourself and no one can stop you.

2. **Find a Secure Place to do your thinking.**
   Most people can't think around a cacophony of noise. They need a quiet place or a quiet time set aside during the day to do their best thinking.

   Solitude has helped many of history's greatest thinkers to organize their ideas. Walden Pond provided a serine environment for Henry David Thoreau to do his best thinking. Don't expect to be able to concentrate on noisy environments with a lot of interruptions. Find your own Secure Place and do your best thinking there.

   Do you write down thoughts that come to you in the night or at odd times? A friend of mine has put a dry erase marker board in his shower because that is where his best thoughts and concepts come to him. Wherever your place is make it a habit to get away and think at least once a week.

3. **Find Some Person to stretch your thoughts.**
   Share your ideas with somebody. Develop a Mind Share Group of like-minded or educated people that you can meet with over the course of this year to share and stretch your thoughts. Build a team around your ideas and thoughts.

   Books are good, as well, but a live person or a group is even better. Aim to read at least one book a month that reshapes your thinking. Do you know that statistics show that only 57% of Americans read an entire book in 2004? No wonder there is no traffic jam on the road to success!

4. **Find Soul Purpose to direct your thoughts.**

What is your vision, your goal, your Purpose? Never stop asking yourself this until you find it. Then latch onto that Purpose and follow it for the rest of your life.

There is a unique reason you were put on this Earth. Find out what it is. Only you can tell. It is your "one thing."

What drives or motivates you to get up and ACT NOW? Do you simply roll over and go back to sleep when the alarm goes off? When you are motivated by your Soul Purpose in life, you will be eager to get out of bed in the morning because you know you'll be doing the things that mean more to you than anything else. You'll be living your Purpose.

5. **Find Superior Power to energize your thoughts.**

Alcoholics Anonymous (AA) grounds its thinking in a "higher power." Most believers see this as God.

Find something bigger than yourself. Look for mentors that will keep you going back to your super-power base.

You will hear people say to avoid shortcuts to success. But there is a shortcut that I will share with you that will get you there quicker.

A shortcut is a more direct route, right? So, what is the most direct route to realizing your Purpose?

The one without any distractions or side tracks. There is a shortcut on the road to your Success and it is the most direct route you can take to your dream -- without distractions or wasted time. Take it!

Use this process to change your life this year. The motivation lies within you to change your life for the better. You must *ACT NOW*, or you will be like so many before you, who put it off until there is no tomorrow.

Barbara De Angelis has said, "No matter what age you are, or what your circumstances might be, you are special, and you still have something unique to offer. Your life, because of who you are, has meaning." Your future is yet to be written. Your thoughts will take you there.

PROFILES

DONALD TRUMP

Donald Trump is known worldwide as a billionaire entrepreneur. Presently, he is also one of the most well-known television stars because of his top-rated show *The Apprentice*.

Although he comes from a privileged background, Donald inherited nearly nothing. He amassed his fortune through his ability to work productively and close mega-million dollar deals. While he has been known primarily for his fame, fortune and love life, you may not know that he lost everything in 1990 and pulled off one of the most amazing business turnarounds in history.

Donald John Trump was born on June 14, 1946 in New York City. His father, Fred Trump, was a successful businessman. His grandfather had died early, forcing Fred into business at an early age. Because Fred had started his own business, Donald learned the tricks of the trade— ways to make deals and increase both productivity and profits -- through assisting his father in the growing business.

Donald attended military school and went on to graduate from the elite University of Pennsylvania's Wharton Financial School. And yet, when Fred Trump died, Donald didn't inherit a large prosperous business. He did inherit his father's ability to recognize a good deal when he saw it, from assisting him in his business for so many years. Donald was ready to become a successful businessman beyond anyone's expectations. Armed with a great education, the experience he'd gained from working with his father and his own in-born ability to negotiate successful opportunities, Donald left Queens for Manhattan.

Although he was almost totally impoverished, he joined an elite business club to make contacts and network with big financiers. The manner in which he joined the exclusive club is a testimony to his ability to negotiate and come out on top. Although the membership was restricted to the wealthy, Donald's reputation had preceded him. He was allowed to join on the condition that he kept his hands off the wives of the other members.

By the 1980's Donald had become one of the most influential and wealthy real estate giants of the decade. He owned or had controlling interest in New York's famous Plaza Hotel (where he even played a bit part in the movie, *Home Alone 2: Lost in New York*), Trump Tower, Trump Parc, the New Jersey Generals' USFL football team, Trump Shuttle Airlines, a 284-foot yacht and several casinos in Atlantic City. You could say he had it all and could only increase in magnitude, but during the recession of the early '90s, Donald lost almost everything.

Donald made most of his deals through loans with major banks. In 1990, he defaulted on them when he could not pay over $1 billion to the banks. Oddly, to his credit, he was able to negotiate deals with the banks and make a remarkable comeback which he discusses in his book **The Art of the Comeback.** He made arrangements for his investors to be paid a majority of their money through the sale of his many properties. In return, it is rumored that they granted him a monthly income, although Trump denies this.

Over the next several years, Donald negotiated deals with people who had liens on his properties and the casinos. By making deals (and getting more in debt), he was able to form a public company, Trump Hotels and Casino Resorts. According to *Fortune* magazine, by 1996, he was carrying over $1.7 billion in debt. He still owns controlling interest in the casinos and several golf courses in New York and Florida.

In 2000, Donald even made a bid for the Presidency. Although unsuccessful, it proved he was back and ready to take more territory.

Today Donald is again successful in real estate, negotiating multi-billion dollar deals internationally and arranging with the financiers to only put up the majority of the money, while he invests only a small portion himself. He is working with contractors an financiers on Trump buildings in Chicago. The Miss U.S.A, the Miss Universe and the Miss Teen U.S.A pageants are his. His television show, *The Apprentice*, is the top show in the 2003-04 season. As a result, he has been featured on the cover of major magazines and attracted a viewing audience that has been absent in recent years from network television. As a result of his television popularity, he hosted NBC's *Saturday Night Live* in early April, 2004.

To hear Donald tell it, he is, and always has been, on top. He will be the first to tell you how successful he has been and how -- even when faced with obstacles that would stall or halt the average person -- he overcame them by his wits and skill. Like him or hate him, you cannot deny that he has the ability to take any situation and turn it into a prosperous and successful one.

People who work for him generally tend to stay with him for years. Understandably, he counts a person's loyalty to him and his empire above all other attributes. It is ironic, then, that the television show has made him famous for the phrase, "You're fired!" It baffles him, since he never thought the board room sessions would become the focal point of the show each week. But Donald has capitalized on it, putting it on poster on the side of his office building in Manhattan and trying to copyright the phrase. Even if he loses everything again and the road doesn't lead up from where Donald Trump is now, you can bet it will eventually through his determination and will to stay on top.

MARY KAY ASH

In the 1930's during the Great Depression, a young Texas housewife and mother began selling books in order to make extra money for the household. Her husband worked, but there was not enough money for their family of five to live on. This woman was so productive in her sales efforts that she was able to sell more than twenty-five thousand dollars worth of books within her first six months on the job.

In 1938, Mary Kathryn, known as "Mary Kay," divorced. She had wanted to study to be a doctor, but since an aptitude test showed that she had a natural strength in selling ability, she took a job selling for the Stanley Home Products company, conducting home sales parties. She kept this job for twenty-five years, even though it was a most unhappy and unfulfilling occupation. She sold very well, but she claimed that her innovative ideas were not appreciated by her superiors.

Another source of discontentment was that Mary Kay felt underpaid and unrecognized when advancement opportunities were available. Often she was skipped over for men in advancement. In 1952, she became a national sales director for the World Gift Company, but found that men she had trained were promoted above her -- at twice her own salary. In 1963, deciding she had had enough and she retired. But only the beginning for the woman would be named "Businesswoman of the Century" by Lifetime Television Network.

Mary Kay's retirement lasted one month! As she began to write a book about her experience as a how-to book to help other women, she asked herself, "Why not me?" She purchased a formulation for a skin-care cream. She enlisted her husband (she had re-married) and her son to handle the business operations and recruited friends to work as beauty consultants for her venture she called "Beauty by Mary Kay." Tragically, her husband died one month prior to launching the new business. Her family strengthened and encouraged her to forge ahead.

On September 13, 1963, Mary Kay Cosmetics was born. In the first year, the business had made almost $200,000. Within five years the company went public. Later, it went private again and today Mary Kay Inc. remains one of the largest privately held corporations in the USA.

When Mary Kay Ash died at 83, on Thanksgiving Day in Dallas, she left 850,000 sales consultants in 37 countries with both the independence that comes from running their own small business and a philosophy of personal achievement that transforms lives. Mary Kay never forgot her goal of helping others and founded the Mary Kay Ash Charitable Foundation, which contributes both to cancer research and to the prevention of abuse and violence against women.

"Throughout her life, the extraordinary thing," says her son, co-founder and CEO, Richard Rogers, "was the way Mary Kay caused people to believe in themselves." Mary Kay's own words live on today through her corporation. She loved to quote Henry Ford and say, "If you think you can, you can. If you think you can't, you're right."

PART III
DEVELOPING YOUR PEOPLE SKILLS

chapter 7

SUCCESSFUL RELATIONSHIPS:
5 KEYS TO BUILDING CONNECTIVITY

"The easiest kind of relationship is with ten thousand
people, the hardest is with one."
- Joan Baez

*W*hat does it take to be successful? I believe that our success is dependent upon relationships -- the connections we make in our day-to-day lives and in business. This includes our families, friends, business associates -- anyone we allow to make an impact in our lives.

Short-sighted people think success is all about themselves. They don't understand the real value of strong relationships. They don't recognize how much relationships contribute to every aspect of our lives. They haven't mastered connectivity.

They may measure success in terms of business, and yet they don't realize that business success is based on relationships too! People have to know, trust and respect you before they will even consider doing business with you.

Relationships are part of the very fabric of our lives. The more effort you spend on building strong relationships with others, the more you will be rewarded with a happy, successful life. So how can you have more successful relationships? The solution is building connectivity with others.

5 KEYS TO BUILDING CONNECTIVITY

1. Successful people understand how their behavior affects others.

Are you aware of the influence you have with other people? To be successful, you need to know that other people get their cues from you.

The reason people treat you a certain way is because of the way you treat them. If you come across too strong, people will naturally either back away or challenge you more frequently. If you treat people with courtesy and consideration, they will respond to you in kind.

Successful people know how to bring the best out in others by their own behavior and actions. What are you doing to develop everyone you come in contact with? What are you doing on a daily basis to develop your strengths to make you a better, more successful human being?

2. Successful people understand their reactions to other people.

You know you are on the road to success the day you realize that you act and react the way you do because you choose to -- not because someone else makes you do it. We constantly hear people saying, "He made me so angry!" or "You're really upsetting me!" as if other people were responsible for their feelings. It may seem like that sometimes, but it isn't true.

Once you come to this realization, you *own* your reactions. After that, you can start to see that, no matter what anyone else does, your feelings and behavior are up to you.

Do you understand how you react to certain people in given situations so that you can always be successful? Are you aware of your blind side enough to know when you are reacting in a negative way to certain people and situations? My advice is to work on your strengths and quit trying to cover up your weaknesses. Examine how you react to certain individuals.

Explore these reactions and find out what is at the root of the negative responses. A quick experiment with different reactions, when someone says something that would've upset you in the past, can show you that your reaction is not set in stone. It's completely up to you. Owning your reactions is an important key to your success.

3. Successful people know how to maximize what they do well.

What are you cut out to do? Where do your talents lie? What are the strengths in your personality style that go best with certain situations? What circumstances bring out the best in you?

Once you begin working to develop your strengths, you need to exercise them in the best possible situations. Know where your "home turf" is. Too many people try to be a "Jack of all trades."

Ronald Reagan was a master at working the camera and inspiring people with his vision. But when it came to carrying out the details of his plans, he delegated them to subordinates he could rely on. Remember when the United States bombed Libya in 1986 and Reagan went to bed? He did this because he had turned the operation over to trusted support staff that could carry out the details of the attack -- unlike Jimmy Carter, who was involved in all the details of both of his Presidential campaigns, because he specialized in details.

To be successful you need to know where you are best suited to excel, then go out and do it. If part of your vision includes skills you don't possess, find good people who can carry it out for you, then delegate. Maximize your strengths and know your weaknesses. Then team up with people who have the strengths you need.

4. Successful people have a positive attitude about themselves.

They know that their attitude is a choice and they make a choice to think well of themselves.

A winning attitude makes all the difference in business today. Successful people exude confidence and build toward a better tomorrow. They are always thinking ahead and motivating others to follow them.

Think about someone you admire most in your life -- perhaps a teacher, a parent, a mentor or a even famous individual who inspires you. I'll bet they have a positive attitude about themselves and they spread the feeling around. It's a universal quality of successful people.

Do you know a good way to check your attitude about you? Look at yourself in the mirror and say, with confidence, "This year I'm going to make a million dollars!"

How did that go? Do you believe in yourself enough that you feel like this is a true statement? Or have you given up? Did some part of you, deep inside, think, "Not me! I could never do that." If you did, you are already discounting yourself and your own ability.

A motivational speaker gave a presentation before a group of prisoners in a Minnesota correctional facility in 1981. He said, "The greatest obstacle standing between you and your success in achieving your goals is you." His words struck a cord with one of the convicts, a young man named Tim Allen, who was so inspired by that vision that went on to become one of the most famous entertainers in the past twenty years. All it took was having a positive attitude about himself and believing in what he could accomplish.

5. Successful people know how to adapt their behavior.

This is what separates the "be's" from the "wannabe's." It is not enough to *only* know your strengths and maximize them. To be successful you need to adapt your strengths and weaknesses, so that you get maximum benefit from every situation.

People often ask me, "Why should I adapt to others? Shouldn't they adapt to me?"

I always answer without hesitation: "Yes. If you don't want to succeed."

If you want the world to revolve around you, I've got news for you: It won't. But you *can* motivate the world to revolve *with you* -- if you learn the skill of adaptation.

For instance, arguing with someone who loves to fight will only hurt both of you. But learning how to communicate without a fight requires mastering adaptation. Every time you adapt to others, you are building skills of connectivity that will make you successful.

As my friend and fellow speaker, Charles Marcus, says, "Successful people realize that every person they meet is an opportunity to make a connection to the future."

Short-sighted people focus on the short-term wins. Smart people focus on the long term and on building a win-win relationship. They build relationships for the future, not just for today.

We live in a world where everyone is looking for quick fixes and instant results. It's a world of high-speed data, impatience with delays and automated connections on voicemail. We all move at a faster pace than our parents and grandparents could have ever imagined possible.

It would be easy to rush past our relationships, as well – to make them as fleeting and disposable as the data stream we live in. But just remember: To become successful, you have to take the time to build relationships that will last.

Successful people are in it for the long term. They know that, no matter how fast our lives become, relationships will always be at the heart of our lives and our success. They use relationships to develop connectivity to bring about long lasting results.

What can you do to start building connectivity -- TODAY?

Chapter 8

THE TOP 10 UNMET NEEDS:
HOW YOU CAN MAKE A DIFFERENCE
BY MEETING THEM

"It is all right your saying you do not need other people,
but there are a lot of people who need you."
- Sherwood Anderson

"*You* can take my factories," Henry Ford once said. "Burn up my buildings. But give me *people* and I'll build my business right back again."

In life and in business, people skills are vitally important. President Teddy Roosevelt knew it. He always said that the single most important ingredient to success was learning to deal with people. A recent study by the Stanford Research Institute revealed that success is 20% product knowledge and 80% people knowledge. Unless you can get along with people, you will never succeed in business or in life.

Even Donald Trump says in his book, *How to Get Rich*, "A certain amount of personal ambition is necessary, but not to the point where it undermines the common goal of the company. If your group can't work together, you won't accomplish much."

But what are people's needs? All of us have different dreams. We want different things in life. Yet, at some level, our basic needs are fundamentally the same. They're human need. We all share them. I've listed the Top 10 Unmet Needs . If you learn to meet these needs, people will gladly follow you for life.

TOP 10 UNMET NEEDS

1. People need purpose.

Knowing what we want in life seems like it should be the easiest thing in the world. But if you asked most people what their Purpose in life is, they would have to make something up. They might come up with an answer, but you'd see from their faces that they weren't really sure. Because most people haven't ever given it any serious thought.

Don Herold said, "Unhappiness is not knowing what we want and killing ourselves to get it." A majority of people rush around, striving for this goal or that, without ever really knowing what they want, much less what their true Purpose is.

That's where you come in. Whenever you can give people a vision that inspires them and leads them forward, you are meeting an important need – one of the most important needs we have.

This is true in your personal life or in business. If you can give your team a vision that is so inspiring, they can't wait to go out and make it happen, they will be eternally grateful to you. You will have given them the thing they were hoping to find in their lives: Purpose -- a way to feel their lives have meaning, that they're doing things for a reason.

Find creative ways to bring a sense of Purpose to the people around you – at home, at social events, at work meetings. Look for humorous ways, fun ways, ways that get people involved and share the excitement with them.

Because I'll tell you a secret: When you are meeting people's needs, you'll not only inspire them, you will inspire yourself and make your own life feel a lot more worthwhile. It is definitely win-win all around.

2. People need to feel appreciated and wanted.

Compliment the people you come in contact with. The highest compliment a leader can receive is one given by his people. The highest compliment the people can receive is one given to them by their leader. The same is true for families. Doesn't it mean more to you when your children are proud of you or your wife admires something you've done? Do the same for them. When was the last time you complimented someone you love? Don't waste another minute. Do it now.

Oh, and don't limit yourself to general compliments. Be specific and people will respond ten times more effectively. Compliment them publicly and you will see an immediate difference. Write hand-written compliments. They go much further than phone calls or emailed messages. Don't you enjoy receiving positive, handwritten notes? Other people do, too.

3. People need security.

Most people are basically insecure. They are insecure about themselves and their own abilities. They lack the confidence it takes to excel. Believe in them.

We all look to others for confidence. Most people on a dance floor are looking at others to see what steps they are using, so they can copy them. We spend thousands of dollars every year on our appearances, so people will accept and like us more.

We all need more confidence. I've heard it said that confidence is that wonderful, uplifting feeling you have before you truly understand the situation. Great leaders provide a secure atmosphere for people in relationship with them, at work or at home.

4. People need to be heard.

Most people have something to say. Everyone has an opinion and should have the opportunity to share it in a safe environment. Listen to them.

We all grew up hearing that "The squeaky wheel is the only one getting the grease." But I like the old Cherokee saying better: "Listen to the whispers and you won't have to hear the screams." Great leaders have their ears to the ground and fingers on the pulse of their people.

If you truly want to be successful, you will go out of your way to meet people's unmet needs, when you can. The best way to find out what someone's needs are is by listening!

5. People need hope.

Give them a vision of a better tomorrow. We all look for a better tomorrow. Ronald Reagan came to the Presidency at a time when American morale was at an all time low. Even his predecessor, Jimmy Carter had characterized the feeling as a "malaise" among the people. But Reagan worked hard to instill confidence and hope in everyone he met. To him it was always "morning in America." His vision inspired the world.

Everyone looks for something better to come. It's what gets us up in the morning. Jane Kerr says, "Hope is the feeling you have that the feeling you have isn't permanent."

When you bring hope to people, you will see the results almost immediately. Find new ways to cast the future in a positive, optimistic manner. Always remember, hope shines brightest when the hour is darkest. In the movie, *Apollo 13* (1995), when the situation seemed hopeless, the NASA Flight Director said, "I believe this will be our finest hour."

Make whatever difficulty your family, friends or workers are facing, inspire them to think of it as their "finest hour." Stand by them and offer them hope.

6. People see the world from their own perspective.

Whenever a problem or change occurs, we all see it from our own perspective which is almost always skewed in our favor. "It's all about me!"

When a change or difficulty occurs, we think it is aimed at us, personally. Remember there are two sides to every question, as long as it doesn't concern you personally.

To truly meet people's needs, you have to realize where they are coming from. And remember, most of us are coming from our own point of view. What could be more natural? We are looking out our own eyes! It takes conscious effort to see something from another person's point of view and genuine maturity not to take things personally.

Train yourself to keep your eyes on the big picture and help other people to see it, too. Recognize how changes and challenges are affecting others on an individual level, as well, and address their point of view. If you care about their concerns, you will meet a very important unmet need.

Everyone will follow a leader who cares for them. Remember the famous Earl Nightingale rule for relationships: "People don't care how much you know until they know how much you care." How much care do you show for the people in your life?

7. People get discouraged.

It's been said that the secret of success is to not let what you are doing get to you before you get to it. It's human nature to lose heart and get discouraged. Some people do it very easily. When that happens, their top unmet need is encouragement. Encourage them. It's easy.

Walt Disney said that there were three types of people in the world. The first group poison other people's lawns with discouragement. The second group mows their own lawn and never leave their yard to help others. The final group, reaches out to enrich the lives of others.

Whenever I give a keynote or after-dinner speech that touches on encouragement, people tell me the encouragement section helped them more than anything else. People need to be lifted up and it doesn't take much time or effort to help them.

Always greet people with a smile and encouragement. You will be rewarded with pleasantness and admiration.

8. People need to be associated with success.

Have you ever noticed how a team that hasn't done very well in years past gathers fans when it is on a winning streak?

I was an Atlanta Braves baseball fan from the time they arrived in town. I suffered through "thin and thin" for years. Then in 1991, they started winning and, suddenly, everyone in Atlanta was a "life-long Braves fan." We called them "Band-wagon fans." Cleveland (baseball) and Tampa Bay (football) experienced the same phenomenon when their teams suddenly gained the winning edge.

We all love a winner. John F. Kennedy described it this way: "Victory has a thousand fathers, but defeat is an orphan." Put a few victories under your belt and you will meet people's unmet need to be associated with success.

9. People need meaningful relationships.

Give them community. Even with the most superior telecommunication systems in history, we are still distant from each other. We can talk more conveniently but we seem to talk less often and with less depth and concern. We move to gated neighborhoods, but still seek community. We share living space, but not our hearts.

Ralph Waldo Emerson said, "The glory of friendship is not in the outstretched hand, nor the kindly smile, nor the joy of companionship; it is in the spiritual inspiration that comes to one when he discovers that someone else believes in him and is willing to trust him." Who believed in you at some point? Who knew you would succeed above all else? Do the same for those around you. Meet their need for someone who believes in them.

10. People need leaders to follow.

Provide people with a great example. Leaders need to know their people's needs and meet them better than anyone else. Your best leadership is by your own example.

In the Time Mastery training seminar I lead for organizations around the world, I show how changing your time habits to good ones is effective in helping you master your time. Showing it to everyone and having them hold you accountable is the best example any leader can give to change the habits of their followers.

Remember that people are always watching you. Don't think you live in a vacuum. Walk around the floor some time and notice how people watch you. The whole world is watching. They are watching for a great leader to emerge. They are looking for someone to follow. It's true at home and at work. I learned this as a father and I practice it in business, as a leader.

Meet these Top 10 Unmet Needs for people every chance you get. Look for opportunities to do it today and watch the results. Within three weeks of constant, need-meeting behavior, you will see a major difference in the people in your life. Not only will they be more productive, but they will enjoy being around you more and you will enjoy yourself more as well. That reaction alone is good enough to try it!

chapter 9

WORKING WITH DIFFICULT PEOPLE:
8.5 PRINCIPLES TO RESOLVING DIFFERENCES

"I'd pay more for someone who can get along
with others than for any other skill."
~ John D. Rockefeller

$\mathcal{S}$urveys show that 58% of Americans like the people they work with. That's nice, isn't it? Until you realize it means that 42% of Americans *don't like* one or more of their co-workers. As I mentioned earlier, it's well-established that good relationships are the key to success. They contribute to our quality of life every single day and to our business success in the long run.

In companies, the accepted formula for profitability reads:

Favorable Work Relations = Favorable Working Conditions = Increased Profits

Everyone knows this is true, yet it's not always easy to ensure favorable working relationships – or any other kind of relationships for that matter. No matter how good our intentions, sometimes relationships are strained because of difficult people.

I've worked in two organizations where certain individuals were being so difficult that it affected every aspect of the other employees' lives. The remarkable thing is that both of these difficult people confided in me that they were behaving badly just to mess things up and see what they could get away with. When others confronted them, they feigned innocence, pretending they were right and everyone else was wrong. But in reality, they weren't even trying to get along with others. They were deliberately being unreasonable and difficult. To them, it was just a game.

In both organizations, there was poor leadership at the top that was afraid of reprimanding or disciplining these people for their disruptive behavior, so the problem continued. The other employees, including myself, were made to suffer because these individuals were allowed to do as they pleased -- unchecked by weak management. People stopped doing their best work, because job performance always goes down hill when people realize that there will be no accountability for their actions.

One person can destroy a business. The same thing can happen in a family. If one member of a family starts acting out and behaving badly, it can demoralize everyone concerned. Steps need to be taken as quickly as possible to put a stop to this behavior.

If you act promptly, though, you can make a difference. The challenge is to take the right steps. Use these solid principles to guide you.

8.5 PRINCIPLES TO RESOLVING DIFFERENCES

1. Who you are will determine how you see others.

We look at others through the lens of our own preferences and prejudices. Look at your own strengths and faults before passing judgment on others. My pastor says that every group has an "Extra Energy Required (E.E.R.) person" -- one who requires extra energy from everybody else. They're also often referred to as "high maintenance." If you don't know who your E.E.R. person is, check the mirror. It could be you.

John Maxwell uses the Bob Principle to figure out where the problem is. If Bob has a problem with John and Bob has a problem with Bill and Bob has a problem with Jane, it's Bob. Bob is the problem.

Remember this: With one minor exception -- the world is entirely composed of other people. You need to learn how to get along with them and get them to put up with you!

2. Know what pushes your buttons.

We talked about this earlier, but it bears repeating. Most people fail to "own" their reactions, so it's easy to push their buttons. Difficult people excel at pushing buttons. Remember, to some of them, it's just a game. Are you going to let them play you? Or are you going to control your own reactions?

You give off signals that tell where your weak spots and vulnerabilities lie. Believe it or not, you've been broadcasting these signals your entire life. I guarantee you that most difficult people already know what pushes your buttons and are probably using it in your relationship to get the upper hand. Get the jump on them before they take advantage of you any further. Know yourself best.

Think of difficult people like sandpaper. They rub on us and smooth out our rough edges. Each person you encounter can teach you something. Ask yourself, "What is the lesson I can learn here? What kind of growth can I get from this relationship?" If you always believe in and look for the best in people, you will find lessons to be learned and growth that will occur in even the worst relationships.

3 . Always *THINK* before you act or speak.

Greg Surratt, Pastor of Seacoast Church in Mount Pleasant, South Carolina, uses this acrostic to help people watch their language.

T   Is it True? Is what you are saying factual?
H   Is it Helpful? Does it lift others up or bring them down?
I   Is it Inspiring? Can it take others with you on the success journey?
N   Is it Necessary? Does it need to be said?
K   Is it Kind? Is it something you want to be remembered for saying? Remember this: Whatever you take in is what comes out when your button gets pushed.

4.   Recognize that you can't please everyone.

As I said earlier, one person can destroy a business. Don't let them destroy you.

Abraham Lincoln said, "You can please some of the people all of the time and all of the people some of the time, but you can't please all of the people all of the time." Here was a man whose entire Presidency was defined in war. Yet he knew how to choose the best advisors and how to bring out the best in some of the most difficult people. He even chose some of his strongest opponents to serve on his cabinet. Sometimes he had to replace people who would not go along with his vision, but he had the guts to make a decision and stick with it, even at the risk of his own career.

5.   Don't get drawn in to arguments.

Keep this in mind: Hurting people usually hurt other people -- and themselves.

When you take a moment to look, it's usually obvious. Some of the most difficult people are lashing out at everyone because they're in pain. Realizing that makes it a lot easier to stay calm around them.

We're often too quick to assume that a difficult person is simply being selfish and egotistical. But that may not be the case at all. Some difficult people are being harsh to push others away, because they expect to be hurt by people as they have been in the past. They're not selfish, they're scared.

If you can find out something about the nature of their pain or at least something about what triggers it, you'll improve your chances of avoiding that wound. Choose your battles and your battlefields. Learn when and where to respond. Know your strengths and your weaknesses so you know how to avoid needless arguments. Arguing is usually the difficult person's home field and they have the advantage.

There's an old saying in the South Georgia that goes: "If you wrestle in the mud with a pig, you'll both get muddy ... and the pig will like it!" It's the same if you argue with a difficult person: You'll both get bloody and the other person just might enjoy it.

6. If possible resolve conflicts quickly and privately.

Don't give a difficult person a public forum to air their grievances or attitude. You only draw others in to a situation that can quickly escalate.

Conflicts are a risk, but I've found that people are worth the risk. Avoid these most common mistakes made in conflict:

- failing to line up the facts;
- being vague about the offense;
- failing to hear the other person's side of the story;
- failing to keep good records;
- harboring a grudge; and
- confronting the other person while you're angry.

Separate what is fact from what is personal and stay with the facts. Like Michael Corleone says in *The Godfather*, "It's not personal, it's business." Okay, don't go and have your adversaries rubbed out, but learn to confront with confidence. Don't let unresolved conflicts fester.

7. Respond in kindness.

Give others what they need -- not what they deserve. And always give people the benefit of the doubt.

Use what John Maxwell calls the 101% Principle. Find the 1% you agree on and give it 100% of your effort. Find ways to communicate in a non-threatening manner that will disarm an aggressive person. Use your communication skills to discover the areas you agree on and foster a mutual relationship of agreement.

Winning together should always follow working together. The only place that is not true is in the dictionary. You always go to a higher level when you take others with you.

8. Go to school on relationships.

Harvard Business School says the Number One Tool for dealing with difficult people is effective communication skills.

Be savvy. How can you stave off outbursts between people? How can you take action that leads to better behavior?

I highly recommend taking a seminar in using tools like the DiSC° Personal Profile System° to help you learn the communications skills you need to better your relationships with all kinds of people. DiSC° is a multi-level learning instrument that shows people how they tend to respond in various situations. It will give you insight into yourself and invaluable advice about how to communicate with other people who have different tendencies than your own. Skills like these make relationships flow much more smoothly. You'll be glad you've learned them. I've never led a group through a DiSC° seminar where their relationships haven't immediately improved.

8.5 Above all, carry a positive image of yourself with you at all times.

Remember, you are valuable and don't deserve cruel treatment.

I was a youth minister for many years in various churches. I learned that if you hold a mirror up to a teenager and ask them what they see, most of the time, they will respond with a self-depreciating, negative comment.

My daughter started Middle School this year and, while I feel her pain as a parent, I am so thankful I don't have to go through that experience again! Older kids can be very cruel to 6th graders. She comes home frequently hurting from what some ill-meaning child said to her on the bus or in the hallway. I soothe her pain, but tell her that she shouldn't let others define who she is. Only she can do that and become a whole, self-aware individual.

The sad truth is that if you hold that same mirror up to an adult, you will often receive the same results. It is sad that we never learned these truths growing up. Eleanor Roosevelt said, "No one can make you feel inferior without your consent."

Be secure in your identity and you will be surprised by how much it decreases your fear about dealing with difficult people. Once you are secure in who you are, difficult people can't hurt your feelings by insulting you.

Your value lies in what you think if yourself. Others -- difficult people in particular -- will set their view of you by the way you define yourself.

chapter 10

CONFRONT WITH CONFIDENCE:
RULES OF ENGAGEMENT

"Confidence is courage at ease."
-Daniel Maher

*W*hen we find that the time has come to confront a difficult person, most of us are at a disadvantage. Aren't we all taught to play nice a get along with on another in kindergarten? Didn't we grow up believing that only mean, scary people confront others?

Even if we wanted to confront someone directly, how would we do it? Most people in the world are decent, honest people, trying to be reasonable. So all we have to do, most of the time, is mention our concerns and they do their best to cooperate. But that's not true of difficult people. The odds are, they're going to have a difficult reaction to our confrontation. That's who they are.

Even confident supervisors and managers at big corporations can be reluctant to confront a difficult person. We are frightened of their reaction.

Think about this, though. Maybe they are behaving in an improper way because no one has ever spelled out what was wrong to them Maybe no one has ever stood up to them in a proper way to confront them. Well gather your courage, take a deep breath and clear your throat. Then apply the Rules of Engagement following. They will allow you to go through the process of confronting another person -- with confidence.

Before you take the first step, tough, there is an important question you must answer:

Are you confronting the other person for *their* own good or are for *your* own good?

If it's about you, you won't get a win-win result. If you are doing it for the other person, you have a better chance of succeeding and bringing about a positive resolution.

RULES OF ENGAGEMENT

1. Clear the air immediately and personally.

Do it now. Don't wait a long time, then "gunny-sack" the other person.

Gunny-sacking is saving up all of your complaints and problems until the bag is full and them dumping it on the other person. Don't get "historical." Getting historical refers to going back over a long period of time and recalling every detail the other person has done that angers you. This will not promote a win-win situation, and I guarantee if it is a win-lose situation, you will lose!

2. Confront with the right spirit.

You must be neither overeager nor hesitant to confront them. The best way to confront is to do it, not because it makes you feel good to vent, but because you are committed to seeing another mature as a human being. Always have the spirit of putting the other person first in the confrontation and you will benefit.

3. Know their personality and behavior (as well as your own).

Different personality types react in different ways to criticism and confrontation. Some people try to change the subject and tell stories. Others tell you what the rules are and go into details. With the proper training, you can anticipate how the other person is likely to react to confrontation and approach them in a way that will make the outcome more successful.

4. Start on a positive note.

Everyone likes to be complimented. Look for the positive things in the other person's actions that you can begin with. This will put them (and you) at ease to carry on the conversation. It is like using an illustration at the beginning of a speech. It gets the other person to think about pleasant thoughts.

5. Outline the problem.

Tell him/her what the conversation is going to be about. Structure what you need in three simple parts:
(1) **What.** Describe what the other person is doing to cause you a problem.
(2) **How.** Tell how this makes you feel.
(3) **Why.** Tell why this is important to you.

6. Encourage a response.

Give them an opportunity to answer to what you are saying. To quote John Maxwell again:

"The people affected are going to feel shock, bitterness and resentment. And they may not spare your feelings by hiding behind a stiff upper lip. Whatever they say or keep to themselves, they won't be ready to listen to the reason this is happening to them until they have expressed their emotion or had time to swallow the hurt."

Keep the subject focused on your concerns, though. Don't allow the other person wander off into another area to distract the conversation. Remember one of the best skills you can use in leadership is listening.

7. Repeat the other person's position.

Re-phrase what they are saying and say it back to them to make sure you (and they) hear what is begin expressed. Allow them to correct misunderstandings or misquotes. Let them know that this is "on the record."

By the way, do not record the meeting without the prior consent of the other individual. Even if they do give their consent, I wouldn't do it, since it has a tendency to put them on the defensive before the meeting even gets started. It's all right, though, to write make notes, and even give the other person a copy for their files, if this is a business setting.

8. Explain why their action was wrong.

Go over the rules that have been broken and make sure they understand what they did that was incorrect. Ask them to repeat or rephrase why the action was wrong. Then rephrase it in their words so they can hear it back. We remember less of what we simply hear and more of what we say and hear.

9. Indicate the desired action to be taken.

This places the focus on the future and minimizes the chances of making the confrontation or the events preceding it "historical" things that get told over and over.

The person who wants to change will gravitate toward the possibility of making things better. This also keeps the conversation on a positive, cheerful note.

By the way, watch out when people say they agree with you "in principle." It usually means they are getting ready to argue or defend themselves.

10. Reiterate the positive strengths of the person.

Go back over their positive qualities and contributions. Emphasize the personal characteristics they have that make you believe they have the ability to change.

Don't bring up anything negative at this point. Remember that you are putting them first in your concern and you want them to be better. The Number One Management Principle is: "What gets rewarded, gets done."

11. Put the issue in the past.

Never bring it up again unless the problem recurs or you use it to affirm positive change and growth. Be careful not to bring it up in a way that makes it seem like you are gloating over a victory you've won. Everyone likes to save face.

After the confrontation, be sure to ask yourself, "Was that really so bad?"

We often imagine confrontation to be worse than it actually turns out to be. Our fears are holding us back. Move forward for the good of the other person. You will find it wasn't as bad as you imagined it would be, and you've helped someone else along the way.

PROFILES

CAVETT ROBERT

We live in a society where the average individual will change professions three or four times in their lifetime. I don't mean jobs, I mean professions. This is nothing new. People have done it for years.

But what about starting a profession that almost no one is practicing? What if there is no model to follow? What if you are pioneering a career in a field that almost doesn't even exist?

Cavett Robert is a perfect example of an individual who changed professions several times in life and went on to great success. He is best known for the one he chose after age 60, a time when most people are looking forward to retirement! He even has an award named for himself. You may have never heard of Cavett, but when you finish reading his story, you will find that you have heard of his many accomplishments.

Cavett was born in 1907 in Starkville, Mississippi. He attended Furman University in Greenville, South Carolina and then the University of Mississippi in Oxford, Mississippi. He graduated from Ole Miss in 1929 with BA and a BS degrees and went to Prairie Point, MS to teach school. He taught first through twelfth grades in this small-town, one-room schoolhouse.

His first job change occurred during his second year. He took a job installing a gas line through the area. After several months, the second change occurred when his brother-in-law, who had just been appointed president of Washington and Lee University, encouraged Cavett to come and study law. Cavett would be an attorney for the next 30 years.

After passing the bar exam, he was appointed a judge in Lexington, Virginia. Following that he went to work with a New York law firm and then with District Attorney (future Governor and Presidential candidate) Thomas Dewey, investigating gangsters and racketeers.

Cavett and his wife, Trudy (a former Miss South Carolina) soon decided that they should move to a warmer climate for their health, so he took a position with a law firm in Arizona which become his new adopted home. He worked for firms in Phoenix, Jerome and Douglas, Arizona.

Arizona Edison Power Company hired him after several years, to travel around to their cities, speaking as a public relations representative for the company at churches, Lions Clubs, chambers of commerce and Toastmasters.

After three years at this speaking stint, he was hired by a law firm in Phoenix to work in their education and real estate divisions. It was there that changes three and four took place, as Cavett got into selling insurance and cemeteries. There were a few other people doing this, but Cavett Robert was the first person to start "pre-need" selling (advance selling of all services for a funeral, so the family would be spared the burden after a loved one's death). He would sell lots in advance for one-fourth the cost. He was so successful that he developed training seminars to educate sales people in selling real estate and cemetery lots. This was the beginning of his sales and training career —change five for Cavett.

Cavett always had a desire to help other people and to speak. He joined Toastmasters International and won the International Speaking Contest in his second attempt. This launched his speaking career. He was also awarded the Golden Gavel Award from Toastmasters International and Speaker of the Year by United Airlines and International Speakers Network.

For the next 25 years, he went around the country speaking. In those days the only professional speakers were doctors, lawyers and politicians. In 1966, he felt a desire to help other people become better speakers with the idea that there was always enough room in the profession for more. The concept of helping each other out in a competitive market was unthinkable. This would be an uphill battle, but Cavett's life motto was: "Don't worry about how we divide up the pie. There is enough for everybody. Let's just build a bigger pie!"

Most professions are so filled with competition, that this thinking isn't rewarded, but to the speaking profession, this would ignite an industry boom -- an industry where very few of the organizations used professional speakers.

He wanted to form a national organization with the goal of making speaking a full-time profession, although no such thing existed at the time. Others had attempted this type of organization with no success. Cavett, though had the desire of helping people become speakers through OPE (Other People's Experience). Only 3% of organizations in that day used outside professional speakers at all.

His first attempt at getting speakers to join his organizations was met with stiff resistance and failed. Speakers would write or call him with discouraging statements: "Oh, it's been tried before ... it'll never work." Remember, these were the people who would one day be known as the motivational speakers we see all around us today!

After a year of discouragement, Cavett realized that he would have to use his skills as a salesman to win people over to the idea of a speaker's association. He had high standards and a clear purpose in mind. The National Speaker's Association was designed to promote high ethical and professional standards of its members. It was never to exist for self-promotion of its members. It was hoped that the public would recognize a member of NSA as one who adhered to the high standards of the profession.

Eventually, Cavett changed his approach. He appointed a board and advertised the high standards to prospective members. They elected the late Bill Gove, a recognized professional speaker, to be the first president and began with sales seminars in Phoenix for eight years. Twenty people joined at the NSA's incorporation. At the fifth-year convention held in New Orleans, 300 people attended -- more than three times the number of any previous gathering.

As the organization grew, it never lost sight of it's purpose. After a few years that purpose became the drive to give an annual award to the individual who embodied the profession's highest standards -- known as the Cavett Award. Cavett, himself was the first recipient in 1979 and Bill Gove was the second.

Today, as a professional member of NSA myself, I can say that our members adhere to strict standards including eight competencies in speaking and training. The association has over 4,500 members and continues to grow annually. There is now an International Speaking Federation for world-wide members.

Cavett passed away in 1997, leaving a lasting legacy in every individual's life who has heard a motivational speaker or trainer from the National Speaker's Association. Personally, we, the members of NSA we call the attitude of helping each other "The Spirit of Cavett." NSA has grown to be a place where people can share, grow and nurture each other just as he dreamed it would. Wouldn't it be great if every profession had this goal in mind?

Next time you think of changing professions, remember Cavett Robert, a man who changed many times and left a legacy of a better world through the encouragement of others.

DALE CARNEGIE

The name of Dale Carnegie is synonymous with success and influence. Yet if you knew his story, you would be amazed that he succeeded at all. Born in poverty on a farm in Missouri, Dale Carnegey (as it was originally spelled) came from humble beginnings. Yearly floods devastated the family farm and kept the Carnegey's poor.

As a boy, Dale was known for one thing: reciting. He used this talent locally in church functions and local events. In high school, he joined the debating team, but never won a debate. He was determined to go to college and attended a state teacher's school. Since he couldn't afford to live at the school, he attended a nearby college and rode a horse to class each day. Because he still loved reciting, he practiced reciting to the horse!

While in college, he heard a Chautauqua Speaker tell his own personal story of triumph and Dale was captivated. Chatugua was an organization known for great speakers around the country. This speaker changed Dale's life. He adopted that speaker's mannerisms, style and voice intonations.

Upon graduation from college, Dale worked at several different jobs. First, he worked as a salesman of correspondence courses, but only sold one. He then he worked for Armour and Company in their lowest-producing territory, South Dakota. Dale turned it into their most profitable territory. But he was making so little money that he was only able to save $500. He decided to use that money to go to New York to take a public speaking course and become a Chautauqua Speaker.

On the train ride to New York, he met a minister who became his traveling companion on the long ride. As they talked, the man advised him to go into acting instead of speaking when he reached New York. Dale followed the stranger's advice, but after many attempts, he only got one role in a play and it was a minor one at that. So Dale decided to quit acting.

It was a difficult period for him. He was so depressed at one point, that he later admitted he had contemplated suicide during this time. But then he remembered his original idea of going into public speaking, Dale gave it one more try.

Since he knew how to recite well and needed to make a living, he applied at the New York City YMCA to teach public speaking, even though he was in New York to learn public speaking himself! The YMCA manager was not overly impressed with him at first and offered him work only if he could get people to take the class at night. The manager also required 80% of his net proceeds. Dale agreed and, at age 24, he was making $2 per night. This became the first night public speaking classes in history at the YMCA.

Dale became such a success that he soon was drawing $25 per session. Within two years, he was making $500 weekly. His ship was coming in! He began lecturing to packed houses. When he was booked at New York's famous Carnegie Hall, he officially changed his name from "Carnegey" to "Carnegie" to help capitalize on the location and notoriety of the more popular spelling of the name (a good lesson in branding). Dale did so and soon proved himself to be a master at taking advantage of opportunities.

As his popularity increased, Dale lectured all over the country and in Europe. He began to write pamphlets on speaking and famous people's lives to sell in addition to his speaking services. After several years, he was able to turn the pamphlets into his first book, Public **Speaking: A Practical Course for Businessmen.** Next, he wrote a book on little-known facts about famous people, similar to and predating Paul Harvey's popular "Rest of the Story" series.

The success of these two works inspired Dale to author his most famous book, **How to Win Friends and Influence People**. It became a bestseller overnight and launched Dale Carnegie to worldwide fame. Dale's book went into 17 editions and made $125,000 within a few months. Most of all, he was helping people overcome their fears and depressions to succeed in life.

He began to do radio shows and columns in numerous newspapers giving personal achievement advice. He also wrote marriage and family advice columns. This prompted Dale to develop one of his trademark themes -- the "assault on worry." He used that theme in his next bestseller, **How to Stop Worrying and Start Living**.

All of his success was built on helping other people find the information they needed to lead happier, more productive lives. Despite his humble beginnings, Dale Carnegie became known as the man who knew how to communicate with and inspire people.

PART IV
Leading the Way for Others

chapter 11

SUCCESSFUL LEADERS:
8 QUALITIES SUCCESSFUL LEADERS HAVE IN COMMON

"Leaders don't force people to follow -- they invite them on a journey."
- Charles S. Lauer

*W*hom do you admire? When you think about models you'd like to follow as you work on your own personal development, who immediately comes to mind? Is it a parent, a close relative, a teacher or a famous historical figure?

Chances are this individual had qualities of leadership that made your admire their strength, their vision and their accomplishments in life enough to want to imitate them in your own life.

When was the last time you thought about this person? What did it take for this leader to make an impression on you? Many great leaders have certain qualities in common. In this chapter, we'll look at eight of those qualities. As you read them, think about a leader who served as a role model for you, but also think about yourself. Do you have these qualities? How would you go about cultivating them?

Personal development begins with helping ourselves and ends with helping others. The more you grow and blossom as a person, the more you have to offer. And, once you begin to offer yourself freely to others, with the best of intentions, you will discover how much joy and satisfaction leadership can bring to your own life.

8 QUALITIES SUCCESSFUL LEADERS HAVE IN COMMON

1. Successful leaders have a positive attitude.

People are attracted to anyone with a positive attitude. We can all go about our lives with a positive attitude. But, in a leader, a positive attitude leads to a positive vision for his people. It can change lives.

In 1991, after Communism had fallen and the Soviet Union had broken apart, a counter revolt occurred. Boris Yeltsin and his loyalists were holed up in the Russian Parliament building as the tanks rolled in the streets.

When one tank approached the building without firing, Yeltsin stepped out and up on to the tank. He reached out and shook the commander's hand. He thanked him for coming over to the side of Democracy. Later, as reporters clamored around the tank commander, he was asked what made he and his comrades decided to come over to Yeltsin's side.

His answer stunned everyone. "We hadn't come over to his side. But when we saw how confident he was, we took a vote and decided to join him."

When you bring a positive attitude to a conflict, you'll be amazed at the results. Even when the people around you can't see the good side of a situation, let your positive vision lead the way. Everyone wants to believe the best can happen. Sometimes all it takes to rally people is one strong leader who holds the flag for change – with their positive attitude.

2. Successful Leaders have something to say.

They don't simply parrot what they've heard someone else say. Leaders apply their knowledge and speak from experience.

Successful leaders can't just sit on the sidelines. They get involved and speak out. People listen to what they say and want to hear more. Managers are leaders because of their position. Leaders are leaders because people want to follow them and their ideas.

Remember the old E.F. Hutton investment firm advertisements of the '70s and '80's. Whenever someone said, "My broker is E.F. Hutton and they say..." Suddenly, the room would fall silent and everyone would lean in to hear the latest tip or words of wisdom. To be a great leader, you must have something valuable to say. When you do, people will be listening.

3. Successful leaders demonstrate passion.

They believe in themselves and their ideas. They know how to demonstrate it before the masses. You can tell that they are passionate about their goals because successful leaders have a sense of conviction. They know where they are going.

For all the self-help books and infomercials on the subject, most people today still have no goals in life. Most of those who do haven't written them down or planned steps for how to reach them. As a result, I tell people in conferences that you can almost stand still and get ahead of the crowd.

Have you ever been so excited about something that you couldn't hold it back? Have you ever been around someone who is like that? Their passion spills over to everyone around them. Do you believe in yourself? No one else will believe in you until you do. Successful leaders have passion.

4. Successful leaders are always learning more.

They are never satisfied with the knowledge they have. They want to know more. They go to conferences to hear the latest trends and come home with the mission to implement more than one that they heard. They want their people to learn more, too.

Every one of *Fortune's* Top 100 businesses to work for in 2005 listed training as one of the most important aspects of success in getting an keeping employees. Great leaders thirst for more knowledge and new ideas. They don't mind asking questions, because they now how to apply the answers to their leadership expertise.

5. Successful leaders are persuasive.

Persuasive people are more prone to become leaders. It's one thing to have a passion and be inspiring. It is a whole different thing to persuade people who don't necessarily agree with you.

Great leaders persuade. They may persuade excitedly or they may persuade through reason, logic, experience and personal charisma. They are articulate and expressive.

Radio talk show host Rush Limbaugh said once that you can have core beliefs and convictions, but you have to be able to express them so that others can understand and follow you. It will always come back around and be of benefit to you. And, it gets easier the more you do it.

6. Successful leaders are aggressive.

They don't wait for action to take place to react to it -- they ARE the action. They assert themselves and take the initiative. They don't just speak out, they lead out.

There is a leadership vacuum in business today. Everyone is waiting for someone to lead the market and their industry. Great leaders don't wait, they are lead the way. As I learned in one of the first leadership conferences I ever attended, "A leader is one who knows the way, shows the way and GOES the way." Assert yourself in the next vacuum that appears.

7. Successful leaders have integrity.

People follow them because they trust them. They have a reputation for reliability and honesty. They don't have an ethics crisis.

I was recently approached by an organization to partner with them. When I checked them out, I discovered that they had a terrible reputation. It's one thing when people tell you to walk away for a bad business deal; it's another thing when they all say RUN!

You will be building your reputation for the rest of your life. Do it wisely. Leave a trail of integrity wherever you go. It will catch up with you one day.

8. Successful leaders inspire others.

Great leaders know that they must not only have followers to be successful, but inspire followers to carry on without them. It you have followers who have grasped your passion and can carry it out, then you have time to turn to the next challenge. This enables you, as a leader to rise to a new level. And great leaders carry their people to the next level with them.

Who are you inspiring? Who wants to be near you to get your enthusiasm and speak for you? Who wants to climb to the next level with you?

chapter 12

A LEADER'S QUICK START GUIDE:
HOW TO BECOME A LEADER YOURSELF

"When placed in command ; take charge."
~Norman Schwarzkopf

*T*hroughout the years, I've had the opportunity to observ great leaders and lackluster ones. We all have. Some people just know how to motivate individuals and others haven't got a clue. Without good leadership, every vision, mission statement or plan will wilt away.

Too often we've seen great dreams reduced to terrible drama as people stumble through the motions in their lives. Don't be that person. This is your chance to excel.

If you become a leader, you will become a tremendous asset to everyone around you – people whose lives are already intertwined with your own at home and at work. You will be in a strong position to share the things you learn on your path to personal growth and developments.

Would you like some quick tips to set your leadership train in motion?

The list below isn't exhaustive, but you may find an area that will improve your leadership ability from say a 6 to a 7 (on a scale of 10). What you put into practice will make a difference in yourself and others for a many years.

QUICK START GUIDE

1. **Great leaders motivate others.**
   Motivation differs from manipulation because of its focus. Manipulation involves getting others to do something for your own benefit. Motivation is getting others to do something for their own benefit.

What you pour into others will stay long after you are gone. Good leaders know that they are only here for a fleeting minute in terms of eternity. It's worth the investment to help others while you're here.

Are you good at motivation? Are you able to get others to do things that make their lives better and more fulfilling? Are people looking to you as a leader because of your past success in motivating others?

2. Work below the water line.

Every leader has a public side that involves the activities they are known for. It's the private side -- what you do behind the scenes -- that makes the most impact.

Imagine an iceberg. Only 20%-30% of it is seen above the surface of the ocean. The great underwater mass is never visible, but its influence keeps the visible part afloat. If you want to be a greater leader, focus your efforts below the water line. As your private influence increases, it will force more of your abilities in the public's eye upward, above the waterline.

What can you do right now to increase the unseen "mass" that is your hidden leadership side? How do you want to be seen in the public's eye? What will it take to do below the water line to increase that vision's visibility?

3. Share the credit.

Share, not the account balance, but the recognition. Good leaders don't care who gets the credit. In the movie, *Remember the Titans* (2000), a racially mixed school's football team is lead by two men: one black and one white. The white coach, Bill Yoast had been coaching successfully for years, but had recently been appointed as an assistant to Herman Boone, a black, successful head coach hired from out of state. In the movie, they must forge an alliance to make the team win and keep the racial tensions from engulfing the team, the school and community.

The two men learn that for the team to win, their personal pride must be put aside. In a key moment of the state championship game, Coach Yoast tells the team that he has learned to look at a man's soul and not his exterior. He then puts aside his pride and asks Coach Boone for help with his defense. The team comes together as the two men have and wins the championship game.

What are you doing that serves only to bring you recognition? Could someone else get the reward and share the glory?

4. Make decisions at the lowest possible level.

At first this seems lazy, until you realize that Moses, in the Bible, had the same problem. At first, he was in charge of everything for his people in the wilderness. He would spend all day judging who did what to whom and where hundreds of thousands of people would eat next. He was in charge of everything from the tiniest detail to the largest needs, i.e., keeping over 400,000 people alive in a desert! Once he learned to delegate, his job became a lot simpler.

The inability to delegate causes burnout in more leaders than anything else. Are there decisions you make that a subordinate or assistant could make? Are you overwhelmed by simple tasks to the degree that you can't handle the large ones effectively? Is delegation a skill you need to acquire to be a successful leader?

5. Handle failure well.

Most people fear failure. The truth is, it can be your best friend, if you know how to use it.

I once knew a football coach who said he was happy with his first loss, because after that, he didn't have the headache of trying to maintain an undefeated season. Our failures teach us a lot about what works and what doesn't. We need to embrace them and learn from them.

Babe Ruth is not only known for hitting homeruns; he also holds the major league record for strikeouts.

The average top CEO has failed seven times before becoming successful. Everyone will fail at some point. Not everyone will learn and profit from it. How can you change your attitude toward failure? What have you learned from past mistakes?

6. Reward growth, but don't punish decline.

Often we are too quick to laud those excelling and put down those struggling. Embarrassing someone never motivates them. We always think of giving public recognition to those who succeed and this is exactly the right thing to do. But good leaders also know how to help the "weakest links," rather than cutting them off.

Look around your life. Is there a way to motivate someone you know who is struggling to succeed? How can you privately encourage them to do better?

7. Evaluate all problems in another light.

Once I sat in on a committee meeting about what color to paint a new building. The fruitless discussion went on for hours into the night. By that time, under fluorescent lights, the paint sample colors weren't showing up as they should, so the group agreed to meet the two days later in daylight to choose the right shade.

The two days did as much to aide the decision as the sunlight. Each person had a chance to think about the big picture and get a new perspective on the task at hand. The correct color was chosen in a matter of minutes.

What problem do you need to stand back and take a look at from a distance of time or perspective? Can it wait for cooler heads?

8. Don't be afraid to ask for help.

Even if you feel you can't talk to someone in your immediate circle, there are plenty of leaders -- consultants and experts -- who are willing to give good advice. Good leaders like to lift up others. The assistance I have received from professionals in the business has been invaluable. It has saved me thousands of dollars and never once risked my image. Pride doesn't make you a great leader. If you're too proud to ask when you need help, how will you lead others to be honest and get help for their own needs?

The movie, *Pass It Forward* (2000), tells of a young boy who develops a program, during a school project of doing good deeds for individuals. The only requirement he makes of those he has assisted is that they pass the good deed forward to someone else.

Who has helped you over the years? Did many people do it for free? How can you pass it forward?

With corporate corruption filling the daily headlines today, there is a greater need than ever for leaders with high ethical standards and integrity -- leaders who know how to motivate and lift up others. In the end, strong leadership will always rise to the top. You can control how high you rise by adjusting your leadership style and practices.

Chapter 13

LEADERS VS. LOSERS:
WHICH ONE WILL YOU BE?

"Show me a good loser and I will show you a loser."
~Paul Newman

*W*hat is the difference between a leader and a loser? As you make your way down the challenging road of personal development, be sure to take the right turns and make the right choices along the way. Some roads look like they're headed toward integrity, vision and leadership, but they are dead ends, filled with people who have made the wrong choices about how to live their lives.

You know what these people look like, when you see them. So do I. At some point, everybody thinks that someone in a leadership position is a total loser. They have been given a position that they are poorly suited to fill.

The other day I got into a discussion with some leaders I meet with on a regular basis about the differences between real leaders and those who are just in a position someone else put them in. We came up with is this list of the qualities of Leaders vs. Losers.

All of us have the capacity to be leaders or losers. In our worst version of ourselves, we tend to act like losers. In our best versions of ourselves, we are definitely winners and even leaders. As you review the list, ask yourself how often you let yourself think or behave like a loser. Think of ways to operate from a position of strength as much as possible, emphasizing your strengths over your weaknesses.

LEADERS VS. LOSERS

- **Leaders think about the next decade - losers think about the weekend.**
A true leader is always thinking several steps ahead of other people. Constantly scanning the horizon for new territory to take and opportunities to seize, they see to the fifth and sixth generations of leadership and how to best influence it from where they are.

It was said that Alexander the Great wept when he marched his army off the known map because there were no more lands to conquer. Leaders want to leave a legacy.

Losers don't want to equip someone else to succeed them. They fear that they will be replaced by someone better. Losers think about how they are going to spend their weekend relaxing and playing. They spend their time in trivial pursuits, wondering what is going to happen to them next.

To excel in personal development enough to become a leader to those around you, you must take charge of your life and make your own choices. Don't wait for life to happen to you, it's time for you to happen to life!

- **Leaders make things happen - losers have things happen to them.**

It's the difference between "'actionary" and reactionary leadership. Leaders see themselves as part of the solution, while losers become part of the problem.

Leadership is all about making decisions that others fear to make. It's about stepping out on faith or your gut instinct and being wiling to take the blame for the results. Loser only want credit for success. Leaders can admit their failures because they use them to learn and move ahead in life.

John F. Kennedy earned worldwide respect when he came on television admitting the failure of the Bay of Pigs invasion. It allowed him to move to a higher level of leadership. Today we have many leaders on both sides of the political landscape who won't admit their failures and then they wonder why people are hesitant to follow their guidance.

- **Leaders see the big picture - losers try to get a snapshot.**

Leaders look over the whole situation and place it in a bigger context. They know their place and constantly try to make the universe a better place through their influence.

It may be lonely at the top, but the view is much better. At the top you can see how one decision affects another and how it will play in your overall vision for the organization. Losers, fearful of doing too much and making waves, take in only sections of the big picture and rarely venture beyond the borders of the matt (much less the frame).

There is a *Seinfeld* episode where Elaine's boss, Mr. Pitt, is unable to see a 3D picture, because he can't focus his eyes correctly. It is a illustration of the mistakes he is making in running the company Elaine works for. Don't be a Mr. Pitt. Get used to looking for the bigger view.

- **Leaders get close to the ones they want to grow –**
  losers distance themselves from their staff.

Frank Lloyd Wright, the American architect. who re-wrote the rules of design in the Twentieth Century, always had the newest apprentices move their desks closest to his own. He wanted them to learn from his example and he poured his knowledge into them. As a result, the success ratio of his staff was far above that of any of his contemporaries.

Why wouldn't you want the new guy or girl to turn out to be successful like you? Losers see everyone as a threat. They think we live in a "dog eat dog" world where no one can be trusted and everyone is a competitor, even people in their own companies or their own families. When friends or family members experience success in their lives, losers aren't happy for them, they are worried and envious. When new people come into a company, a loser will not offer them assistance and encouragement, but will force them to work their way up.

There is no need to fear the success of the people around you. We are all learning and growing all the time. And there is plenty of room at the top. Keep people you can help close to you. It will not threaten you, but enrich you.

- **Leaders develop healthy relationships with people -**
  losers "date" people looking for the like-minded.

Leaders know that you can't inspire people who aren't close to you. If you were going to find someone to dedicate your life to, would you bar-hop until you met the right person at a glance or spend your time building relationships with individuals to deepen the commitment level? Organizations are too full of people dating prospects and failing to build relationships.

As my friend Don Hicks in Missouri puts it, "There is a difference between having sales and having clients." Sales leaders develop deep, healthy relationships on which future business can be built.

Losers go from one job to the next just trying to stay alive. A friend of mine has a sign in his office that reads: *"I don't have to survive, I can thrive!"* Are you thriving or surviving? The relationships you build will help you to thrive and grow for years to come.

- **Leaders inspire - losers perspire (then expire).**

You can always tell leaders by their vision and the followers it gathers. It is said that if anyone who claims to be leading has no followers, he/she is merely taking a walk!

Look behind you once in a while. Is anyone following? Are you able to motivate everyone by your vision?

Duration is an important element of leadership, since the longer you are with people, the more they can reflect on what you have done for them and come to respect your value to them. At this point you have risen to a new level of leadership.

Losers inspire no one and eventually run out of steam. They have to function on dry hot air. In the last days of the American Revolution, when his generals were trying to revolt against congress, George Washington was able to inspire them to put their trust in him and his leadership and fight on. A true leader can rouse his followers even under the most dire circumstances. A loser can't get people to follow him even under ideal circumstances.

- **Leaders think positively - losers think negatively.**

Most successful leaders know they are in their position because of the dominating positive thoughts that are in their minds, not because of their accomplishments.

If you are resting on your laurels, be careful that they don't wilt under the pressure of your ego. Henry Ford challenged his engineers to develop an 8-cylinder motor when the concept was unheard of. Time and time again, they came back to him saying it was impossible. But Henry would stubbornly say, "Go back and try again." He was convinced that it could be done and nothing would deter him. Eventually he was proved right by the same people that spent their time thinking of ways it couldn't be done.

How about you? When a new dream or proposition lands at your feet, do you think of ways to make it work or ways it won't? A positive attitude will make all the difference.

- **Leaders are confident - losers are insecure.**

People who try to rigidly hold onto the same position don't hold it for long. Their insecurities become evident and they lose followers. If you are spending your time reinforcing yourself you will quickly run out of support and supplies.

The great generals have always been known for the territory they took and battles they won, not the things they did when no one was fighting. Leaders know their strengths and abilities. They know their weak points and how to compensate; how to put the right people in the right places to cover the gaping holes.

A loser wants all the credit for themselves in a vain effort to reinforce their role as "leader." But it is a hollow title for someone who lacks the qualities of leadership.

- **Leaders are role models - losers "phone it in."**

Leaders know the way. They live the way. They are the way. They are at the forefront, modeling what they want their followers to do. Losers are hiding in the background waiting for someone else to take charge.

Mahatma Gandhi and Martin Luther King, Jr. believed in peaceful resistance. They led out front. They modeled what they believed in and it still inspires millions today. You never saw them hiding in a room, while their supporters marched or protested. They were out front resisting peacefully, no matter how violent their adversaries became. When Hitler's Third Reich was crumbling, he retreated to a bunker, where he took his own life and died the death of a coward.

When times are tough, a true leader will model the behavior and attitude they teach. They become a walking, talking picture of what they want their followers to become.

- **Leaders generate motivation – losers generate stagnation.**

Leaders empowered with a vision know how to go to all the right people and spread that vision. They approach individuals and groups, looking for discontent with the status quo and use that to instill a desire for change.

Losers prefer to maintain the status quo. They are the ones who came up with the phrases: "If it ain't broke, don't fix it" and "We never did it that way before." They fear the unknown and usually hope someone else will step up and take the reins, so they can quickly get out of harm's way. Losers don't want to talk one-on-one for fear that they will be discovered as lacking the ability to lead. Nothing grows and everyone goes – away.

- **Leaders embrace failure – losers avoid failure at all costs.**

Frank Lloyd Wright frequently spent months and years, experimenting with ideas that ultimately failed. "How else can you succeed, unless you try something new and learn from it?" he asked. More of his designs were built than those of his two top architectural rivals combined. He pushed his apprentices to learn from their mistakes.

When they would write to him from overseas job sites about difficulties they faced saying, "How do you solve X problem?" he would wait several weeks then write them back with the reply, "How did YOU solve X problem?"

Only through repeated trial and error do you learn and grow. Losers are so afraid that they will fail that they risk nothing, learn nothing and fail to grow. Are you allowing your people to risk failure at all?

- **Leaders listen to others –**
  losers talk about themselves and their accomplishments.

Mark Twain once said that a wise man says nothing; the fool talks and reveals to everyone he is a fool.

Leaders know that they must constantly hear new ideas from people who have never had an opportunity to share them with anyone before. Your greatest skill in leadership is the ability to keep your ear to the ground for trends, ideas and opinions. Listen more than you talk and you will learn more. Talk more and others will quit talking to you.

Presidents Abraham Lincoln and John F. Kennedy surrounded themselves with advisors that were smarter than they were in areas they knew nothing about, so the two men would get the best advice when he needed it.

Do you want to take the next step in your personal growth? Do you want to be a leader? Be a risk-taker. Defy the status quo. Succeed through others. Keep spreading your vision. As my friend, Joe Bonura says, "You will succeed in direct proportion to your desire to come out of your comfort zone."
Lead on!

PROFILES

STEVE JOBS

"Innovation distinguishes between a leader and a follower."

Steven Paul Jobs began life as an orphan, adopted by Paul and Clara Jobs of Mountain View, California in February, 1955. When Steven was unhappy in school in Mountain View, the family moved to Los Altos, California. Even there, he was characterized as a loner with a different way of looking at things.

While in high school, Jobs showed a genuine love for technology and attended Hewlett-Packard seminars. After school, Jobs attended lectures at the Hewlett-Packard electronics firm in Palo Alto, California. There he was hired as a summer employee. Another employee at Hewlett-Packard was Stephen Wozniak, a recent dropout from the University of California at Berkeley, who was an engineering whiz with a passion for inventing electronic gadgets. The two teamed up to market ideas. Steve graduated from high school in 1972. He then attended one semester of college at Reed College in Portland, Oregon before dropping out.

In 1974 Steve became a video game designer for Atari, Inc., a leader in the electronic gaming and recreation industry. He was not really interested in creating electronic games, but his passion and innate ability for marketing these products was the defining moment of his life. He approached his friend, Wozniak, to help him build a personal computer. Using capital from selling scientific calculators, the two set up a production line. He convinced his friend to quit his job with Hewlett-Packard to become the Vice President of Research and Development for the new enterprise. They named the garage-started company "Apple," after a summer job Steve had had working in an Oregon orchard.

One of Jobs' great achievements in those early days was reducing the personal computer to the size of a small box. It influenced the Xerox Corporation to re-introduce their idea of the mouse. Many companies used Apple's interface to develop their own software. Their crowning achievement during this period was the introduction of the Apple MacIntosh Computer on Super Bowl Sunday, 1984. It competed with the IBM personal computer.

As the years went by, other executives at Apple began to force Steve into less influential roles and he found himself being pushed out of leadership in the company. One day, in 1985, Steve surprised everyone by stating, "I've been thinking a lot and it's time for me to get on with my life." He resigned from Apple and began a new company that developed computer hardware, called NextStep. There, he continued his forceful way of creativity mixed with hard-nosed perfection.

Steve's drive for perfection often led him to be ignorant to other people's ideas. One ex-employee recalls how Jobs was so demanding that, on principle, he would often reject anyone's work the first time it was shown to him. NextStep proved to not be as successful as Steve intended, so in 1993, he eliminated the hardware division of the company and concentrated on software development. His software was paired with Intel's 486 processor, but most consumers preferred other operating systems.

In 1986, Steve purchased George Lucas' animated division of Lucasfilms film company. Steve then turned his attention to developing animated feature films that might rival industry leader, Disney Studios. The new company was called Pixar. In 1987, it produced its first feature-length film, *Toy Story*. The movie was ground-breaking in its style of animation and special animated effects. It broke box office records. It was soon followed by other record breakers: *A Bug's Life, Toy Story 2* and *Monsters, Inc.*

With each new film, Steve's company not only set new records, but changed the face of animation. For instance, there was a cherished industry belief that only Christmas releases would succeed. Steve didn't believe it and to prove it, he released *Finding Nemo* in the summer of 2003. It was a smash hit. The industry maxim was thrown out the window.

Steve helped launch the personal computer revolution with the introduction of the Macintosh, the first graphical user interface operational system we are now so used to, as well as introducing the mouse and laser printer to the general public.

After a very public exit from the company he loved and founded, Steve returned triumphantly in 1997 to rescue a struggling Apple and turning it into the vibrant company it is today. He began with the development of the revolutionary iMac personal computer.

Steve soon became interested in music as a new marketing vehicle. When asked why he never became involved with the handheld computer device (PDA's), he said that if you go back hundreds of years, you find people in business not looking for methods of data entry, but loving music. Steve wanted to find a way to bring music to everyone through computer technology.

Internet companies like Napster and Kazaa had revolutionized music file-sharing, but had done so illegally. The music industry was hurting from free file-sharing, so Steve sought to find a method of internet music downloads that satisfied both the artists, the industry and consumers. This led to the birth of the iPod, Apple's revolutionary digital music player.

At first only a few music companies signed on, but eventually Steve secured contracts with the five major music production companies. First, the iPod played songs, then it displayed photos, then podcasts. Most recently, Apple released the latest iPod which allows consumers to download not only music files, but music videos and television programs from ABC/Disney. The company says it will change the way we experience music and more. Steve said at the introduction, "We will see how the consumers use the new device to drive future development."

Steve lives with his family in Silicon Valley, the area of Southern California that was transformed from an apricot orchard into what was once known as the creative center of computer technology. He is a visionary in the world of personal computers and has changed the industry from top to bottom.

The moment there were rumors that Steve Jobs was returning to Apple, the stock price shot up almost 100% in value. His charisma is unrivaled. When he speaks at a MacWorld convention, his onstage presence has the crowd greeting him with standing ovations, then listened intently to his every word. If a businessman's talent is measured by his success, Steve Jobs' talent is unsurpassed. His ability to transform Apple from a company that was losing $1 billion a year into one that makes over $1 billion a year is enough to prove his worth and to demonstrate why he is hailed as a genius.

STEVE MARTIN

Steve Martin has become one of the world's best-known comedians. Oddly enough, he started out studying philosophy and wanted to become a college professor in the subject. He is a member of Mensa International, an organization whose members have IQs in the top 2%.

Ultimately, though, Steve dropped out of college to pursue a career in comedy writing. He started writing for numerous television shows before going solo as a stand-up comedian. He is known for his ability to come up with ridiculous twists that have launched a great comedic career and numerous world-renowned catch phrases. Stephen Glenn Martin, born August 14, 1945, is an American comedian, writer, producer, actor, musician and composer. He was born in Waco, Texas and raised in Orange County, California. As a boy, he worked at Knott's Berry Farm and Disneyland in concessions. Steve credits this with the beginning of his love for entertaining. At these amusement parks, he developed his skills in playing the banjo, lassoing, juggling, making balloon animals and improvisational comedy.

About his years studying philosophy at California State University at Long Beach, he .once said, "In philosophy, I started studying logic, and they were talking about cause and effect, and you start to realize, 'Hey, there is no cause and effect! There is no logic! There is no anything!' Then it gets real easy to write this stuff, because all you have to do is twist everything hard. You twist the punch line, you twist the *non sequitur* so hard away from the things that set I up, that it's easy... and it's thrilling."

In 1967 he got a job through a girlfriend writing for *The Smothers Brothers Comedy Hour,* for which he won an Emmy. Later his comedy writing skills went into shows like: *The Ray Stevens Show, The Glen Campbell Goodtime Hour, The Sonny and Cher Comedy Hour* and *John Denver.*

Though he liked writing, Steve wanted to perform on stage, so he honed his comedy act and opened for various rock bands. By the end of the 1960's, he was performing his own material in clubs and on television. As Martin appeared in front of more people, his popularity rose. He made several appearances on *The Tonight Show with Johnny Carson* and his fame went nationwide. His style was off kilter, bizarre and ironic, often poking fun at stand-up comedy traditions.

Steve went on to host several shows in the innovative *Saturday Night Live* series. He, in fact, holds *SNL* records for most guest appearances, most times hosting and most times hosting the show in one year (3). He starred in and co-wrote four highly rated television specials. When performing on national concert tours, he drew standing-room-only audiences in some of the largest venues in the country. He won Grammy Awards for his two comedy albums, *Let's Get Small* and *A Wild and Crazy Guy,* and had a gold record with *King Tut.*

The Nitty Gritty Dirt Band had formed a friendship with Steve during his opening act days and they appeared on *King Tut,* calling themselves The Toot Uncommons. An accomplished banjo player, he appeared in Earl Scruggs and Friends on the *Foggy Mountain Breakdown* video, for which he won a Grammy for Best Country Instrumental Performance. This is a rare achievement, since Steve has won Grammies for both comedy and music.

Steve took the comedy world by storm, coining catch phrases like: "Excuuuuse me!", "Wild and crazy guy," and "Let's get small." After that, he made his move into films.

Steve's first film project, *The Absent-Minded Waiter*, a short movie he wrote and starred in, was nominated for a 1977 Academy Award. In 1979, he moved into feature films, co-writing and starring in *The Jerk*, directed by Carl Reiner. In 1981, he again starred opposite his girlfriend, Bernadette Peters, in Herbert Ross' bittersweet musical comedy, *Pennies From Heaven*. The actor then co-wrote and starred in the 1982 spoof of detective thrillers, *Dead Men Don't Wear Plaid* and the sci-fi comedy, *The Man With Two Brains*, both directed by Carl Reiner. In 1984, Martin received a Best Actor Award from both the National Board of Review and the New York Film Critics Association for *All of Me*, with Lily Tomlin and his then-wife, Victoria Tennant. Steve starred in several other comedies with veteran comedians: *The Three Amigos* and *Planes, Trains and Automobiles*, with the late John Candy.

Wanting to avoid being type-cast as a buffoon, Steve wrote a contemporary remake of the play, *Cyrano de Bergerac*, called *Roxanne*, and played the lead opposite Darryl Hannah. His role in *Roxanne* won him a Writers Guild of America award. He went on to star in *Parenthood*, with Goldie Hawn. Then made *House Sitter*, *The Out-of-Towners* and *Cheaper by the Dozen*.

At the same time, he actively worked to establish his intellectual credentials by writing articles for *The New Yorker*. A collection of these articles were published in book form as **Pure Drivel**. As a playwright, he authored *Picasso at the Lapin Agile*, which had a successful run in several large cities.

Returning to the Hollywood scene, he hosted the 73rd Annual Academy Awards in 2001. In 2003 he was listed as #50 in *People Magazine's* "50 Most Beautiful People" List.

Steve Martin is a testimony to doing things your own way with a certain style, even if your style is off-the-wall. His success has been steady and almost always in whatever direction he set for himself.

A long-time art collector, Steve is also a trustee of the Los Angeles Museum of Art, and collects the art of O'Keefe, Diebenkorn, de Kooning, Kline, Twombly, Frankenthaler, Hopper, Hockney, Lichtenstein, and Picasso. He summed it all up himself, "I think I did pretty well, considering I started out with nothing but a bunch of blank paper."

Some of his most memorable quotes are:

"I wrote a novel this year called **Shop Girl**, and several producers came to me and wanted to turn it into a movie. And I said, 'If you think you're going to take this book and change it around, and Hollywoodize it and change the ending ... that's going to cost you.'"

"All I've ever wanted was an honest week's pay for an honest day's work."

"Chaos in the midst of chaos isn't funny, but chaos in the midst of order is."

"I believe entertainment can aspire to be art and can become art, but if you set out to make art, you are an idiot."

"It's very hard being one of the most beautiful people. Having this kind of beauty is actually a burden. Sometimes I go to a party and not one of the other 49 most beautiful people is there. That makes me feel very solitary and alone, because it means I am the most beautiful person in the room. If I'm going to a party where I know there will be 'less-beautiful people,' I try to 'dress down' in order to hide my beauty. But this seems to have a counter-effect of actually making me more beautiful. I guess me and dungarees are a pretty potent combination. I try not to lord my beauty over others. This is very hard. I try not to mention that I am one of the most beautiful people, but somehow it always comes out. I will usually only bring it up when I'm asked to do a task, like open a garage door. People seem to enjoy my beauty and are genuinely happy for me, because after I mention it they always say, 'How nice for you.'"

PART V
Achieving Excellence

chapter 14

MAKING EXCELLENCE ROUTINE:
7 MILESTONES FOR YOUR JOURNEY

"You are what you repeatedly do.
Excellence is not an event -- it is a habit."
-Aristotle

*E*xcellence is a rare experience. It can be defined as doing the right thing at the right time in the right way. It has also been described as "a journey without end."

Many corporations, such as Six Sigma, LEAN and others, are using modern methods to make that journey. The Oakland Raiders football franchise has long posted signs on their stadium that read: "Commitment to Excellence."

What does it take to commit to excellence in our lives, in our work and with our families? Wouldn't it be a great feeling to know you take pride in your productivity and can chart your own course to excellence?

Here are Seven Milestones to use on your journey to Making Excellence Routine:

1. **Resource Use.** Eliminate wasted time, space, labor, information and steps. Learn to work smarter, as opposed to harder.
Many speakers today say, "Work smarter, not harder," but I like what Ronald Reagan said best, "It's true hard work never killed anybody, but, I figure, why take the chance?"

2. **On-time Dependability.** Do what was promised when promised in production, service and other functions.

Woody Allen says "Eighty percent of success is showing up," but I say, "One hundred percent is showing up first." No one remembers when you got it done -- unless you were late. You've probably seen a cartoon in print shops that have a bunch of characters laughing with the caption: "You want it when?" Be the one who can be depended on to deliver.

3. **Unwavering Flexibility**. Make a rapid response to changes in the market-place and customer demands.

Companies that have stayed on the cutting edge are the ones that believe in responsible flexibility above all else. A friend of mine in Atlanta calls it "responsi-flexibility." That's a good name for a simple action.

4. **Teamwork Development.** Make maximum use of each person's abilities in the right position on the right task.

A Human Resources department is a key asset of any company, yet many struggle day-in-and-day-out with the same HR problems and never seek to develop their most important asset: people. In the end, everything is done by people, made by people sold by people and used by people. Don't waste them in any phase.

5. **Innovation.** Always advance in production and process.

I remember growing up in Atlanta and seeing the slogan on Southern Railroad boxcars as trains went by: "Southern gives a green light to innovation." It always makes me think about how many companies have gone under while Southern merged with Norfolk Western and expanded. Companies that give "green lights" to innovations and welcome them meet the demands of the market and consumers.

6. **No Defects.** Maintain an internal quality control that has zero tolerance for defects, makes a rapid identification and quickly corrects errors.

Baby Boomers grew up with "planned obsolescence," but we have shifted to low tolerance for mistakes in a competitive world. As long as your rivals can do it better with fewer mistakes, they will defeat you in the marketplace.

I once saw a basketball t-shirt that said it all: "Somewhere, someone is practicing right now. And when you meet him in competition, he will defeat you." Always be prepared more than your competition.

7. **External Quality.** Please your customers. Develop relationships with your customer base and service their needs promptly.

Our van once got stalled in Florida just before we were to board a cruise ship. The local Chevy dealership not only repaired the van while we were gone, but delivered it at no extra charge to the parking lot where we would arrive when we got back. They went out of their way to please their customers. It's a good policy.

Clark Howard, a consumer radio talk show host, refers to most customer service departments as "Customer No or Dis-Service." Sadly, I think he's right.

I called the customer service hotline to get my lawn mower repaired last year. When I asked the customer service rep on the other end why their number was not published in the owner's manual, he responded, "We really don't want people to call us all the time." Enough said!

These Seven Milestones offer you a simple way to make excellence routine. You don't need to create an earth-shaking new product or provide a service so amazing, it keeps people up marveling all night. You just need to do a few simple things reliably and well. Do that, and it will set you apart from your competition and keep you on the road to excellence.

Chapter 15

PROJECT PROFESSIONALISM!:
12 EASY STEPS TO BEING MORE PROFESSIONAL

"Professionalism is knowing how to do it, when to do it, and doing it."
-Frank Tyger

$\mathcal{T}$oday's business world demands more than ever before. Competition is intense. Wouldn't you like an "edge" over everyone else?

That edge is Professionalism. It is a MUST if you are going to succeed in the marketplace today. Supervisors today are scrutinizing budgets with great intensity to see where the excess "fat" can be trimmed. Techniques such as Six Sigma and LEAN are emphasizing better production, less mistakes, with fewer workers and more profits as a result.

In the '90's, it was "in" to look more casual. Many people took advantage of that dress code to start *behaving* casually in their business dealings. But in the new millennium, it's back to business suits. Yes, like the '80's, "it's 'hip' to be square (again)."

But what does it take to project a professional image? What are the marks of a true professional?

Here are 12 easy steps to being more professional . Work on one each month and you'll find that by the time the next year comes along, you will have adopted a very professional presence with your co-workers and your customers.
P: Positive Attitude. More people are hired and fired because of their attitude. In study after study, inadequate workers who get along with everyone are retained longer than those who don't.

Attitude is everything. Decide tomorrow morning that it is going to be a *great day*, then watch your expectations come true!

In fact, if you take the letters in ATTITUDE and assign their number in the alphabet to them (A=1, T=20, etc.), you will find that they total 100. Attitude counts for 100% of your image and success! As your attitude changes, your altitude in life will increase. (Check out www.jimmathis.com/AIA.pdf to read about a workshop that your company, firm or association can hold to improve attitudes at work and home.)

R: Reliability. This is an earned reputation for doing what you say you will do, and on time, too. I lived in South Florida in the mid-'90's and the service industry in my town was terrible. Why? Because many people went to the beach on sunny days. (Most days in South Florida are sunny!) If you needed something, the service workers knew you couldn't call anyone else to repair or install your services. Try that in Atlanta, Minneapolis, New York, Chicago, Charlotte or anyplace where people want the business and you'll be out of business! Even in South Florida, reliability is a business practice that is treasured because it's so rare!

O: Organization. Can you find your notes, your schedule and your contacts with little effort? How does your workspace look? Do you project an image of clutter or organization? The next appointment you miss or show up late for may be the one that takes your business down. Trust me, people are watching you. Use Outlook, ACT!, Maximizer or some other contact management system. Learn to prioritize.

A quick way to start organizing is to make a list of what you need to do, then take your top ten items and circle the top two. Concentrate on them and the rest (the other eight items) will take care of themselves. Try it! (For more information, go to: www.jimmathis.com/TimeMastery.pdf.)

F: Flexibility. This naturally follows being organized. Once you are organized, flexibility will be easier for you.

Rigidity in today's market can kill you. Businesses that are unwilling to change with the times are being left in the dust every day. The day when Henry Ford could offer only black Model T's is laughed at in the market of the new millennium. Stay on schedule and on your mission, but be willing to show some flexibility in dealing with people. They will respect you for it in the long run.

E: Even temperment. How well do you handle stress? Do you bring problems home with you from the office? Do you bring problems to the office from home? In a competitive market, no one wants to deal with extraneous problems on the job. The art of coping is a learned art and required of all professionals. It is increasingly hard to concentrate on the job when there are terror threats, warnings and an unstable market/economy. Those who can't cope are left by the side of the road to success.

S: Speaking Positive. Speak positively to everyone. Watch your speech. How do you convey yourself? Can you express even negative comments in a positive manner? Instead of pointing out what you won't do for customers, learn to express the things you will do.

Focus on the positives! Be the first to complement someone. Practice on waitresses and cashiers. You'll be surprised at their response and it will give you the reward to do so more often.

S: Self-awareness. Professionals know their personality and behavioral styles. They know how they can be most effective in relationships with co-workers, clients, and customers. They also know what they need to work on in their character to be successful.

Use the DiSC Classic Assessment (www.jimmathis.com/DiSCTeamwork. pdf) to evaluate your strengths and weaknesses. As Clint Eastwood's character says in *Magnum Force*, "A man's go to know his limitations." A woman does, too, Clint!

I: Staying Informed. Are you staying on the growing edge? Do you seek new ways to educate yourself in your profession?

There are many opportunities today that didn't exist just ten years ago for self improvement and continuing education. Check out the local college, tech school, or other extension educational services for classes to learn more. Go to the library and see what they have to offer. If you haven't been recently, you'll be surprised at the books on audio you can check out for free a listen to on your way to and from work. Use your down time as growth time. Ben Franklin said, "When you're finished growing, you're finished."

O: Objectivity. Can you look at every situation with an objective eye? Can you put yourself in another person's place? Professionals know how to look at the problem from every angle. Supervisors and CEOs alike enjoy having someone close to them who can objectively look at ideas, problems and solutions.

The old practice of being surrounded by "yes men" is passé. Today's market requires problem solvers who can look five steps done the road and two steps ahead of the competition. They need the advisors around them to make a contribution to that, rather than obscuring their view by agreeing with everything they say. The more you can do to generate true objectivity, the more of an advantage you'll have in the marketplace.

N: Neatness. The casual '90s were fun and many businesses still have casual Fridays. But if you want to get and keep business in a competitive market today, you have to look more than just competent. It's back in style to "dress for success." Don't buy the cheapest suit or dress you can for the office. Spend the money where people will notice your appearance and give you their business. Again, people are watching you!

A: Accountability Are you a man or woman of integrity? How well do you handle money (corporate and personal)? Does the boss know where you are when you are on the clock? Are you giving your best effort on the job? If you aren't, it is already showing.

Practice keeping your co-workers and supervisors informed of where you are on a project. Don't be afraid to ask for help. It is better to ask for help now, than for references tomorrow because you failed on an important task.

L: Listening skills. How well do you listen to others? Do you know how to ask "listening questions?" These are questions that seek more in-depth information – the ones that don't require a "yes/no" response.

Do you make a practice of taking notes in a conversation? Often I've found this practice keeps me from dominating the conversation and allows the other person to not only speak, but feel like you are hearing what they are saying. Everyone wants to feel that they are important. Hearing someone out is a great way to tell them that what they are saying is important to you.

Do you know how to restate the other person's comments back to them to clarify what was said? This also reinforces their importance and your comprehension of their message.

(For more information on how to improve your Listening Skills,
go to: www.jimmathis.com/Listening.pdf.)

By cultivating and honing these skills, you will continually improve your level of professionalism. It's a quality that will allow you to make a greater impression on the job and in your life, as well.

chapter 16

THE FOUR LAWS OF ENHANCING SALES:
THE ART OF ADAPTING TO SELL MORE

"Sales are contingent upon the attitude of the salesman -- not the attitude of the prospect."
- W. Clement Stone

*D*id you meet all your sales goals last year? What are you doing to do a better job this year? One of the keys to achieving success is understanding the art of
adapting. Because we live in a time when changes are taking place at a faster pace
than ever before, adaptation has become more important than it was in the past.

Did you know that there are Four Laws of Enhanced Selling? If you apply
these laws, your ability to build on your success by continually adapting will grow
and your efforts will be rewarded. Don't wait! Read them now and start selling
more!

Law #1: You cannot motivate other people. No one wants to be sold.

Admit it: You didn't wake up this morning and say to yourself, "I hope someone sells me something today." We all shy away from slick telemarketers. It's why
we dread going to buy a car. Unfortunately, most sales people don't realize this.
They can't wait to make their sales pitch. When their pitch succeeds, they think
they've motivated people to buy. But that's not what's happened. You cannot motivate other people.

What you can do is meet people's needs. It all starts by asking great questions. What are great questions? Great questions don't require a "yes" or "no"
answer. They are questions that make the prospect talk about themselves and their
needs.

A friend of mine had an assistant for several months who made his calls to
prospects for speaking presentations. She would call the prospect, say she was calling for him, then tell them everything he did as a speaker. Well, you can imagine
the response she got – none. My friend suggested that, instead of telling what he
spoke about, she might start asking them questions.

Soon people were talking to her. They were telling their needs, their problems and, most importantly, what kind of speaker they wanted to hear. My friend's list of prospects grew almost immediately.

What if you went to a car lot and the salesman asked you about your lifestyle? Instead of asking you what type of car you wanted, what if he asked you about your family? What if he listened to you and pointed you – not to the car he wanted to sell, but to the car you actually needed?

Too often salesmen are simply looking for a way to exploit our emotions. When we buy something that way, we are sold based on the emotion of the moment. Seth Godin, marketing guru, says in his latest best seller, <u>All Marketers are Liars</u>, that if we all bought with our brains instead of our emotions, we'd all be driving Hondas. I don't know if it's that drastic, but he makes the point that we often are forced into buying the wrong thing without thinking about what we really need.

Law #2: All people are motivated.

I know this seems to contradict Law #1, but bear with me.
Simone de Beauvoir said, "Buying is a profound pleasure." Everyone likes to buy. I just said no one wants to be sold, right? But that's not the same as buying! Learning the difference between selling and buying will put you way ahead of most sales people.

Buying is fun. We love to buy. We love to get a "deal." It's in our psyche that we like to shop around and look at all the models, all the options, all the bells and whistles. Go to an outlet center sometime and you will see that people love to buy. Look at the business E-Bay and Amazon do every year. People *love* to buy! They'll buy things that end up sitting in the corner out of the way, while they wonder why they ever wanted such a worthless contraption. That's because they *didn't* want the contraption – they wanted to *buy it!* In the moment, the urge to buy can be so strong! Don't believe it? Go to a neighborhood yard sale and look at what useless things people are buying.

If you understand this, you have a leg up on the competition. All you have to do is find out how to allow people to buy from you without trying to "sell" them to death.

Go to woot.com and see how they allow people to buy. This is a creative website that sells only one item a day for 24 hours, then takes it off the market. You can't get it from them, even if you beg them, after the 24 hour deadline. They sell cutting-edge electronics and gadgets at rare discount prices. They have almost no customer service. It is very hard to contact them to return something. Why? The company is run by just two guys -- two very creative guys.

So how can you use your creativity to get people to buy without trying to sell them? Ask your prospect questions. Then ask them more questions.

Who is in charge of the conversation, when one person is asking questions? You got it, the Questioner. Give your prospect option that they can choose between to get a better deal. Find ways to let them enjoy the buying process. It will be to your advantage.

Law #3: People do things for their own reasons, not your reasons.

Everyone likes to buy in their "comfort zone." What is their comfort zone? It is where they live. It is where their strengths lie. It is in their personality and communication style. A talkative person doesn't like to be sold by a demanding, bottom-line sales person. A bottom liner doesn't like to be sold by a meek, wimpy sales person. We all like to speak our own language and be spoken to in that same language.

Think about the last time you bought something from a sales person that was a good experience. They made you feel special, didn't they?

Think about the people you buy from regularly. Chances are, they allow you to buy in your comfort zone, without being "sold." Realtors experience this law most often. They show house-after-house to prospective buyers, but nothing happens until the family finds "the right one." When they do, the family feels at home and is motivated to buy. Why? They are buying to suit their needs for a home, not someone else's.

Law #4: A person's strength, when overused, may become a limitation.

In other words, you can't sell something from your comfort zone. You must allow the buyer to buy in their own comfort zone. If you can master adapting to other people's styles, you can work with anyone to allow them to buy in their own comfort zone. Start by asking great questions. Listen to not only *what* the buyer is saying, but *how* they are saying it.

Sadly, too many sales people try to push for the sale at the expense of adapting to the buyer's needs. My good friend and expert sales trainer, Joe Bonura says, "You will succeed in direct proportion to your willingness to come out of your Comfort Zone." Maybe you haven't met with success because you have stayed in your comfort zone too long. Get out now and beat the competition. The further out you go from your zone, the more successful you will be.

Try out all these laws out on your next sales call. Even if you've been having good success, if you haven't been applying these laws, you can improve it! You will see the difference in your first conversation with a prospect. People react extremely well when salespeople apply these laws. Your results will be visible in a very short time!

PROFILES

GENE HACKMAN

Gene Hackman's life is a testament to rising above unfortunate circumstances, overcoming early setbacks, defying the critics, finding what you want to do and pursuing it with all you've got. Once you read his story, you will see that persistence is necessary on the road to success.

He was born Eugene Alden Hackman, on January 30, 1930, in San Bernardino, California. A child of a broken home, Gene ran away and was raised by his maternal grandmother in Danville, Illinois.

Arrested for stealing candy and soda from a convenience store, Gene had become something of a problem, when at the age of 16 he decided to drop out of school and lied about his age to join the U.S. Marines. He served in China and the Pacific, but left the service at the end of his third year to pursue a career in radio, a talent he had learned in the Marines. Upon his discharge, he enrolled at the University of Illinois to study Journalism, but left to go to New York and pursue his dream of doing radio. During the 1950s, Hackman studied at New York's School of Radio Technique and worked at several radio stations in the Midwest.

He had planned to make radio his career, but when he attended a showing of "Streetcar Named Desire," starring Marlon Brando, that all changed. When they left the theater, he told his father that he wanted to be an actor. This became his lifelong dream and fueled his ambition.

Gene moved back to California and enrolled as a student at the famous Pasadena Playhouse in Los Angeles. While at the Pasadena Playhouse, Hackman and another classmate were voted "Least Likely to Succeed." The classmate was Dustin Hoffman.

He was given a 1.3 out of 10 ranking at the Pasadena Playhouse, but he was determined to prove them wrong. In 1956, he headed to New York to work on stage. That same year, he married Faye Maltese, and together they had three children.

After landing appearances on television shows and a small role in his first feature film, he finally had his first substantial movie role in *Lilith*, starring Warren Beatty. This led to Hackman's breakthrough performance in 1967's *Bonnie and Clyde*, for which he earned an Oscar nomination for Best Supporting Actor, portraying Clyde's brother Buck Barrow.

In 1971, Gene finally scored a leading role, earning great reviews and an Oscar for Best Actor, as New York policeman Jimmy "Popeye" Doyle in *The French Connection*. In the 1970s, he racked up a string of memorable performances in hit films, including *The Poseidon Adventure*, *The Scarecrow* (his favorite role) and *Superman*, in which he starred as the villainous Lex Luthor.

Hackman once said, "If I start to become a star, I'll lose contact with the normal guys I play best."

The story is told that in 1974, he called Mel Brooks and asked if there was a role in the comedy *Young Frankenstein* available for him. Mel cast him as the inept blind peasant, Harold. In that movie, Hackman ad libbed the now famous line, "Hey, where are you going? I was gonna make espresso!" It took several takes to get a shot without Mel Brooks laughing in the background.

By the late 1970s, the filming schedule had exhausted Hackman, and he took a brief sabbatical from acting, returning in 1981 in Beatty's *Reds*. In the early 1980s, he made less successful film choices, but he was one of the busiest actors in Hollywood. His career was revived in the latter half of the decade, with *Hoosiers*, *No Way Out* starring Kevin Costner, and *Mississippi Burning*, for which he received his third Best Supporting Actor nomination. His marriage to Faye ended in divorce in 1986. In the early 1990s, Hackman underwent surgery for heart problems, but he continued to work.

He initially turned down the role of Sheriff Bill Daggett in Clint Eastwood's acclaimed Western, *Unforgiven*, because he thought little of Westerns. His performance though, finally garnered him an Oscar and Golden Globe for Best Supporting Actor.

He married Betsy Arakawa in December of 1991. In the latter 1990's Gene settled comfortably into a rhythm, alternating between lead roles and high-profile supporting performances. His more recent films have showcased the broad range that he has displayed throughout his career, such as the corrupt lawyer in *The Firm*, the angry submarine commander in *Crimson Tide* (co-starring Denzel Washington), and Eastwood's *Absolute Power*. In sharp contrast, he also starred in comedies such as *Get Shorty* and *The Birdcage*.

In 2001, Hackman impressed everyone with his performances in three very different films: *Heist*, the war film *Behind Enemy Lines*, and *The Royal Tenenbaums*, for which Hackman earned a third Golden Globe award.

In 2003, he received the Cecile B. DeMille Award for "outstanding contribution to the entertainment field." It was a fitting tribute to a man who has portrayed many varied characters for almost four decades. That same year he starred in the critically acclaimed *Runaway Jury* followed the next year with the light-hearted comedy *Welcome to Mooseport* co-starring Ray Romano.

Hackman often says he wants to quit acting in films, but that every time he has time off away from the set, he starts to miss it and wants to start another film. He revealed on Larry King's television show in 2004 that he had no movies lined up. When asked why, Hackman replied by saying that he thinks it is the end of his career.

Whether he has come to the end of his career or not, Gene Hackman has shown us what we can do when we set goals in life and put everything we have into meeting them. He has made a career as a successful character actor whose uncommon abilities and smart choices have ultimately made him a leading man. Gene Hackman's life shows without a doubt that persistence does indeed pay off.

SUZE ORMAN
"Being rich is one thing, but being financially free is another."

Born in Chicago, in 1951, this daughter of working-class Russian-Jewish immigrants has become one of the world's most well-known and popular financial advisors.

Many people don't realize that this famous public speaker was born with a severe speech impediment. So bad was her speech that it affected her reading ability. In the elementary school she attended, children were seated according to their reading scores. While Suze's friends who could read well and got superior grades sat in the front of the room, she was placed at the rear, which further hampered her grades. Fortunately, she scored high marks in math and science, which would prove helpful to her later in life.

One moment from her youth was especially pivotal. At thirteen, she watched her father rush into a burning building to retrieve his cash register. As he dropped the burning hot machine, she saw the skin from his arms and chest fall off with it. The lesson of the importance of money stuck with her.

Although she went to college, she dropped out because of a learning disability in English – a result of the speech impediment. Instead, she traveled cross country to California, where she secured a job as a waitress in a bakery in Berkeley, earning $400 a week. Suze had dreams, though. She dreamed of owning her own hot-tub and spa next to her own restaurant. A friendly woman, she shared her vision with her most loyal customers. One day, a friend handed her a no-interest loan for $2,000, to be paid back in ten years. As other customers contributed over the next few months, she amassed $50,000 and set about to fulfill her dream.

Suze knew she had to take the money and put it to work for her and her dream, but she had no knowledge about investing. She took the money to a brokerage firm which advised her to put it into the volatile oil market. The first few weeks she saw an exciting 10 percent gain, but it quickly turned around and she lost all of her money. Devastated, she panicked over how to pay off her investors.

Eventually, the brokerage firm took responsibility for the failure to secure her money, but it started her asking questions about whether she could do a better job with her own money than she could by paying someone else to do it. Exploring the idea, she first took a job with the same brokerage firm, but found she disagreed with their business practices, so she started her own financial investment firm, The Suze Orman Financial Group. Soon she was making money on her own and investing for others with her growing knowledge of financial markets.

Everything seemed to be going Suze's way until the day she showed up for work and found out that all of her records and money had been stolen by a former employee and business partner. Computer files, software, client records and contact information had all been taken from her in the middle of the night. Once again, she found herself broke and destitute.

During this period, she experienced another epiphany when went to a restaurant and saw a waitress carrying on her duties with great joy. It reminded her of her days in the Berkeley bakery. The happiness of that young waitress touched her and made her re-think her values.

Suze turned to religious thought and went inside herself to find her spiritual home. She realized that God had a purpose for her life. She started talking about the spiritual side of success and financial freedom. She felt that everything that had happened in her life had been a gift that she was to be grateful for, rather than embittered by.

"The lesson I learned was that my attitude toward money had made me poor and that with that attitude, no amount of money could have made me rich. Money doesn't bring courage, I learned. It's the other way around. Once I took the lesson to heart, I began to rebuild my life." Her spiritual approach to finances influenced her advice to her clients. She told them to get out of debt, avoid expensive purchases and free themselves from the use of credit cards.

This is the message of her best-selling books: **You've Earned It - Don't Lose It, Nine Steps to Financial Freedom, The Courage to be Rich, The Laws of Money, The Lessons of Life and The Money Book for the Young, Fabulous and Broke.** Suze's popularity allowed her to sell her own PBS financial specials, make appearances on Oprah, write articles for *Self* magazine and eventually win an Emmy Award for her television show on

CNBC cable network. She has amassed a fortune and developed a financial organization that makes over a million dollars annually.

By all accounts, her humility in the midst of her success remains intact. Although she maintains three residences -- a home in Berkeley and apartments in New York and in Florida -- she says she eats out only twice a week and cooks at home most days. She makes a point to donate 25% of her annual proceeds to charity and still sends money to her mother.

Suze says, "I love the feeling of being wealthy, but I am in shock about it. When my first book came out, I used to stand outside bookstores and ask friends to go in and see if the book was on sale. Of course, it wasn't, most of the time, so I'd ask them to go back in and order it. Even now, I don't like to go into bookstores and don't watch myself on TV. Success is a kind of facade to me in that way."

The message in Suze's books and her television appearances has transformed the lives of millions all over the world. Her basic message is: "People first, money second, things third." She has survived being poor and wealthy several times in her life, but she has learned to get the maximum benefit from her spiritual wealth.

PART VI
COPING WITH CHALLENGES

chapter 17

TRYING TO REASON WITH HURRICANE SEASON:
LEARNING TO COPE WITH BAD EXPERIENCES

Every problem has in it the seeds of its own solution.
If you don't have any problems, you don't get any seeds.
-Norman Vincent Peale

*J*une 1 is the beginning of Atlantic Hurricane Season each year. It ends all too mercifully November 30. Living on the East Coast of the United States, I am directly affected by hurricane season. My friends in the Heartland or the West deal with storms of a different nature --mudslides, tornados, earthquakes and floods, etc.

Last year, friends in North Dakota talked to me about the difficulties of their blizzard season. Hawaii seems like paradise, but residents there are constantly under the threat -- not only from hurricanes and volcanoes -- but from earthquakes that can result in deadly tsunamis. In recent years, we have become all too aware of their impact and unpredictability.

No matter where you live, storms will come in your life -- physically, emotionally and spiritually -- and you will be called upon to cope with them.

When I speak on this subject before audiences, I talk about seven familiar TV characters whose lives were upset for over 14 years by a single storm. Those of you who can remember or who have watched old TV reruns, will know I'm referring to the passengers of the S.S. Minnow from the '60s TV show, *Gilligan's Island*. Although we laughed at their problems, they always reminded us that everyone, regardless of their station in life, is affected by storms.

Hurricanes, earthquakes and tornados are categorized to label their intensity. For the sake of our discussion, we'll categorize storms that come in our lives, so we can explore some ways to cope when bad things happen.

Category 1 - Storms that you create. These are troubles of our own making. We can't blame them on anyone else, because the culprit is in the mirror. Here are just a few examples: "I forgot to fill the gas tank. I invested everything in dotcom stocks in 2000. I got caught speeding. I started smoking and quit exercising. I took on more than I could handle at work."

Category 2 - Storms that someone else creates. These are storms that are the fault or others. I once had a '66 Mustang that I was restoring. It was about 85% restored when I went out one morning to find it was gone. Someone had stolen it. At times, dealing with the police and insurance company was a bigger hassle than losing the car! I hadn't left the keys where someone could take them. I had locked the doors. But a classic Mustang is tempting bait for an auto thief. Later that year, our house was broken into and all of my wife's jewelry was stolen.

Both of those storms were Category 2. Someone else had created them. But a pattern was emerging. My wife and I figured that if we hung around for someone to steal from us a third time, it might put us over into Category 1: A storm we created by staying. Since we were renting our apartment, we got the message and moved. Sometimes it's good to get out of the natural path of storms!

Category 3 - Storms that come in the natural order. Tornados, floods, earth-quakes, and hurricanes are what insurance companies call "acts of God." But when you come down to it, it's our choice to live in certain areas that are prone to some natural disasters (If you want to insure against get shark bitten, don't leave Kansas City). Many people hate their jobs, but what they hate just comes with the territory. If you can't cope with it, leave. That's right, leave. Life is too short to be miserable doing what you don't enjoy. If you don't want to leave, find ways to make it pleasurable.

Category 4 - Storms caused by evil. These occur because there is evil in this world. There is evil in terrorism, in illegal drugs, in disease, etc. Ask any police officer, nurse, paramedic or emergency room doctor and they will tell you they have looked into the eyes of evil on an almost daily basis. Look at the people around the world suffering because of diseases, human trafficking, theft and wars.

We don't often choose when bad things happen, but we can always choose how we react to them. Your reactions to these storms are keys to overcoming bad occurrences in life.

In the '60s, there was a baseball pitcher named Clem Labine, who had had a broken finger that was set improperly. When the bone grew back wrong, he was told he would never pitch again, but Clem was determined to prove the critics wrong. Through discipline and practice, Clem developed one of the best curve balls in the major leagues. Only he could throw it due to his physical defect. He had turned a storm into an asset.

FACING HURRICANE SEASON

So what can you do to face your own Hurricane Season with confidence and a positive outlook?

Here are a few things that have always worked for me. I highly recommend them.

1. **Guard your time.** Learn to say "no" to interruptions. Do positive things in your spare time. Read and listen to things that will build you up rather than bring you down. If it is negative or harmful, ruthlessly delete it from you life and routine.

The two most precious commodities in life today are money and time. You can make more money, but you can't create more time. You can only change your priorities, so that more time is available to you to get things done. Live a life prepared for the times when you will need your faculties to face difficulties.

2. **Read more than you watch TV.** This single action will turn your "influencing" factors in a positive direction. I watch educational and entertaining things on TV, but for me, reading will never be replaced as the best way to improve my outlook on life and build me up when the storms hit.

Did you know that less than 60% of Americans read "at least one book" in 2004? No wonder we see people caught up in bad circumstances. They don't reach out for the information they need to cope with the storms in life.

3. **Save money.** Start or improve your savings account. I know several individuals who, when times were prosperous, spent all they had. When the storms hit their lives, they had nothing to fall back on.

First, I pay 10% of what I make to God. Then, I pay the next 10% to myself for savings and retirement. If you can't live on the remaining 80%, you need to earn more or cut back on your spending.

When I was 12 years old, the Boy Scouts taught me how to face storms in life with the motto: "Be prepared." It's a motto simple enough for a boy to understand that we can all apply for the rest of our lives.

4. **Learn from the storms.** When life knocks you down, find out why. Use bad experiences as storm warning lights. Find out what can you learn, so that when it happens again, you will be better able to face it. Be careful, because, if problems don't make you better, they may make you bitter. Which way will you go?

Only a fool will repeat his mistakes knowing the outcome will never change. Who do you know that went through a disaster and never got over it? Do you envy them or see where if the same thing happened to you, you could improve yourself.

5.   Remember that you are more in control of your life than others are. This simple thought will keep you from playing the "blame game." Quit blaming God for your lack of success. Odds are, you might have been able to move ahead, but were too busy blaming God, nature or society for your problems. The world's most successful people aren't defensive or insecure. They rise above their circumstances to succeed. Only you can control your schedule and your reactions to others. Start exercising your authority over your own life.

6.   Ignore people who try to discourage you. These are miserable people who are jealous of your dedication to a positive, fulfilling life. Jim Stovall, founder of the Narrative Television Network, tells about how he became blind as a teenager and had to give up his life-long desire to become a football player. When he came up with the idea of a TV network that narrated scenes for the blind, he got more negative criticism than he had ever imagined he would. After getting over his surprise, he simply ignored the critics and went ahead with his plan. Today, he speaks from experience, when he says, "If you ignore the critics, they will go away eventually and bother someone else." Try Jim's method and see if it works for you.

7.   Make it a habit of helping others. Get in the habit of helping out when storms come into other peoples' lives. Give blood to the Red Cross. Volunteer your spare time to help a humanitarian group, like the United Way. See what community mission project you can get involved with through your church.

This will help you, first, in knowing how to cope with storms through your efforts. Second, it will build a support group around you who will come to your aid, when storms hit your life. Third, it will help you keep life in perspective. Helping others in crisis reminds you that life is full of storms. They come over us all indiscriminately. Giving to others in their time of need will help protect you from self-pity or despair in your own times of need comes. You will know only too well that they happen to all of us and, together, we can survive. Everybody at some point experiences a storm in their lives. You are not alone unless you choose to be.

8.   Make positive selections. This sounds easy, but in reality, the world is more than half negative. Make it a habit of finding and choosing the positive.

I wear a piece of jewelry around my neck every day to remind me to see the positive side of every circumstance. It's my own Positive Amulet. I use it to remind me that it can hang face down, with its best side covered, or face up, as it should be.

Earl Nightingale wrote in *The Strangest Secret*, "You become what you think about all day long." These words were the ones that influenced him. They are the words that continue to influence me and will influence you. Remember them. The next time storms come into your life, choose your reaction. It may be the defining moment that turns your life around in the right direction.

chapter 18
MAKING FAILURE YOUR FRIEND

"Failure is a part of success.
There is no such thing as a bed of roses all your life.
But failure will never stand in the way of success if you learn from it."
-Hank Aaron

*N*ot only will storms inevitably sweep through your life and wash your success overboard from time to time, but at some point, you will also meet with failure. If you are very fortunate, the failure will not be extreme. But even if it is, you are in good company. Some of the greatest success stories in the history of the world were achieved by men and women who had suffered abject failure and made it their friend.

Most school children can tell you how the American Revolution began. We've all learned about the battle of Bunker Hill, "No taxation without representation!" and the first shot "heard 'round the world" in Concord. Most historians will tell you that the French and Indian War planted the seeds for the American Revolution. But do you know how the French and Indian War began? It was a war that engulfed Europe for seven years and cost the British crown one of its most valiant generals.

It seems the French were inciting Indians in the Ohio territory to raid and kill English settlers in the mid-1700s. The King of England dispatched a squadron of troops and allied Indians under the command of a young, untested major.

As soon as he arrived in the Ohio territory, a minor skirmish took place and major's forces captured the leader of the French. While the young major discussed surrender terms with him, one of the allied British Indians unexpectedly struck down the French official and killed him.

Several weeks later, the French sent in an overwhelming force to conquer the British and force a surrender. The young major was forced to sign a formal surrender written in French. He could only read English and thought the document said that he simply surrendered his post. Actually, the statement was a confession that he had personally murdered the French official in cold blood.

As a result of the major's unwitting confession, France declared war on Great Britain, launching the Seven Years War in Europe (known as the French and Indian War in America). Britain won, but not without paying a high cost in expenses and in the lives of its soldiers. Ultimately, France ceded Canada to Great Britain, but the cost of the war forced the British government to raise taxes on the American colonies. Those taxes led Americans to revolt. It was launched, as you know, at the Boston Tea Party with Paul Revere's famous midnight ride.

But whatever happened to the young British major who confessed to a crime he didn't commit? Disgraced and humiliated, he was never assigned a prominent command again. But he was so desirous to serve in battle that he attended the First Continental Congress in his militia uniform, hoping to catch the eye of the delegates and gain a command. He was successful in this attempt. He was given command of the entire Continental army and later of a fledging nation. His name was George Washington.

After beginning his career with such a devastating failure, George Washington might have been forgiven for skulking off quietly into a corner, hanging his head in shame. In fact, the King of England virtually told him that was the best that he deserved. But as we know today, Washington was made of sterner stuff.

Not only did he become an extraordinarily successful general, beloved of his men, but a great leader in our nation's history, and the first president of the United States. Few of us will experience success of that magnitude, but we can all learn from our mistakes and turn our failures into success.

There are two things to keep in mind.

1. Everyone is going to fail.

Quit trying to avoid a loss. A football coach I know once said that he was glad to lose his first game because it took the pressure of a perfect season off his shoulders. He was taking failure and making it his friend.

Everybody fails at some point. Learn to anticipate failure with a positive attitude. Mother Teresa called failure "the kiss of Jesus" on her life and looked forward to what her failures could teach her.

It's well-known that Babe Ruth, a hero to baseball fans, also holds the major league record for strikeouts. Mickey Mantle, one of the greatest hitters in the history of baseball, went to the plate without a hit so many times, it was the equivalent of seven full seasons! You are never so close to victory as when you are defeated in a good cause.

2. Everyone can learn from failure.

But not everyone knows this. They fail, cover it up and try to act like nothing has happened.

Did you know that Ivory Soap is the result of a chemical flaw? It isn't pure soap, so it floats. Rather than discard the results, they used it as a marketing campaign. The advertisements for Ivory Soap proudly proclaimed that it was 99 44/100% real soap. The rest is air. And, as a result of the little bit of air that is in the soap, Ivory floats. They failed in the lab and turned it into an advantage.

History says that George Pickett, the Southern General who led the famous ill-fated charge at the Civil War Battle of Gettysburg never got over the loss. He blamed it on Robert E. Lee the rest of his life. We all know people who choose bitterness and despair over recovery after a failure.

There are even fewer people who turn failure into their greatest success. You can be among them. You may not be able to choose the outcome of events. You may not even be able to avoid failure. But you can choose to make failure your friend.

When life shuts a door in your face, look for the window of opportunity you can crawl through. We can overcome our failures and move on to greater things. History teaches us this lesson repeatedly.

One of the secrets to making failure your friend is not losing heart. If you start to lose sight of the fact that failure is an event that happens to everyone and start thinking it's who you are, you're putting yourself in great danger. Confederate General George Pickett couldn't stop thinking of himself as the general who lost at Gettysburg. If he had thought of it as a single, important battle or even a single, devastating failure, he would have had a much better chance of moving on.

There is an enormous difference between saying, "I failed," and saying "I'm a failure." If you think you are a failure, it will be much harder to expect success of yourself in the future. Change your phrases. Change your attitude. Most people don't see you as a failure unless you project that image.

One of Washington's favorite generals was Benjamin Lincoln. Lincoln was a New Englander and a good commander. He fought bravely and successfully at the Battle of Saratoga. Washington gave him command of the forces at Charleston, South Carolina (the fourth largest city in America at the time). Lincoln attempted to take the port city of Savannah, Georgia, from the British but was repelled back to Charleston. Several months later, General Henry Clinton, of His Majesty's Army, forced Lincoln to surrender his Southern Department and the city of Charleston.

This was a terrible failure. It was the largest surrender of American personnel during the war. Lincoln would be known forever for this failure he suffered. Lincoln admitted he'd failed, but he did not wait out his captivity thinking, "I'm a failure." He continued to believe in himself.

Six months, later he was freed in a prisoner exchange and immediately rejoined Washington on the Hudson River. Less than a year later, he assisted in the Siege of Yorktown. At the surrender of the British, Lord General Cornwallis refused to be present for the official ceremony of surrender. He sent a subordinate to give his sword to George Washington. Washington refused to accept the surrender from a subordinate and appointed Benjamin Lincoln to accept Lord Cornwallis's sword. This man who had overseen the largest American defeat of the Revolutionary War was elevated to "hero" by officially receiving the British surrender and the end of hostilities.

This would have come as no surprised to Washington. He had failed in his own first command, by overcoming that failure, he went on to become the "father of his country." The most pivotal people in the history of our nation have often lived lives plagued with failure. The founders of both Ford and Honda automobile companies failed numerous times before attaining the successes they are famous for. These men credited their successes to their failures.

The question is not, Are you going to fail? You are going to fail. That fact is certain.

The question is, What are you going to do with your failure? Will you mope in self-pity and dismiss yourself as a failure or will you turn that failure to your own purposes and make it your friend?

Use each day as an opportunity to seek out the lessons failure can teach you and turn your deficits into dividends for success.

chapter 19

C.H.A.N.G.E
TO DEAL WITH STRESS:
LEARNING TO COPE WITH BAD EXPERIENCES

"Seek not to change the world,
but choose to change your mind about the world."
-A Course in Miracles

No one will argue that we live in a stress-filled society. It's hard to tell if it's more stressful in this generation than any before. But one thing is certain: each individual thinks their problems are worse than everybody else's! Studies indicate that air traffic controllers have the most stressful jobs, but that doesn't stop people from feeling their own jobs are worse. Is that how you feel?

You don't have to be an air traffic controller to be familiar with stress. All of us encounter stressful situations on a daily basis. To deal with stress we need to focus on four areas:

1. **Problem Solving**
2. Communication
3. Closeness
4. Flexibility.

Then take the six steps in this chapter to make the CHANGE.

If you are wondering how well you deal with stress, here are some questions to ask yourself: How is your problem solving ability? Do you put things off, separate people from the problem, separate out emotions, have a desired outcome? How well do you communicate under stress?   The amount of closeness we feel with others greatly affects our ability to cope. Do you make relationships a priority? How flexible are you? Are you open to diverse ideas?

Below is an acrostic using the word "CHANGE" to help you develop an action plan to deal with stress. The six letters in CHANGE anchor six important steps for making and maintaining positive movement in your life.

C: Commit

Commit yourself to a specific goal. Set an attainable goal that helps you deal regularly with the stressors of life that lead to tension and anxiety. For instance, you might want to improve your communication skills at work by using reflective listening. This involves paraphrasing the speaker's ideas to the speaker's satisfaction.

H: Habits.

Break old bad habits and start new ones. Decide today that the bad habits of the past are just that, the past. For instance, focus on future goals instead of dwelling in the past. Often we are diverted from our goals by problems in the present. Keep both eyes on your personal, work and family goals. Don't let anything deter you from focusing on them.

A: Action

Take one step at a time. Do something today! Take "baby steps" with your actions but start your new action plan right away. For instance, read a book on self improvement. Start your new habits now by taking a friend, colleague or family member out to eat and practice your new plan.

N: Never give up

Lapses might occur. Every book I've ever read about marketing says to never give up on your marketing plan. When we back off from our direction or goals, we forget and apathy sets in. If you don't succeed today, try again tomorrow. Winston Churchill gave a speech at a commencement exercise that is widely quoted. In it, he said: "Never, never, never, never give up."

G: Goals

Be goal-oriented. Focus on the positive. Look at ways you have advanced your plan, not the ways you have failed. For instance, get a close friend to affirm your actions. Keep the eventual goal in sight. Start praising yourself for what you can do, not what you can't. Mary Kay Ash, founder of Mary Kay Cosmetics said, "If you think you can, you can. If you think you can't, you're right."

E: Evaluate

Be sure to evaluate and reward yourself. Once a week, do something for yourself to mark the progress you've made. Treat yourself to something special. Do an activity that brings you great feelings for the goals you have accomplished. Give yourself a "bonus" for a job well done.

The CHANGE model format is appropriate for developing Action Plans in each area of life. Refer to it as an ongoing guide for creating positive change, and keep looking up!

PROFILES

TIM ALLEN

Few people know this, but Tim Allen (born Timothy Allen Dick in 1953), television and movie star, best-selling author and philanthropist, was once imprisoned on drug charges. He was in prison in Minnesota in 1980, when he heard a motivational speaker deliver a message that changed his life.

Tim had always wanted to be an entertainer. In fact, in prison, he organized a stand up night so he and the other inmates could enjoy comedy. Of course, he performed as a part of the program each night. He knew that he wanted to go into comedy, but he had always faced roadblocks that had stopped him. Being incarcerated was another major roadblock to his career --or so he thought. The speaker he heard spoke about goal-setting. He told the audience that success was in their grasp. The only obstacle they faced was themselves and their own attitudes. This message hit home with Tim. He realized that, in fact, he was the only stumbling block between himself and his life goal.

When Tim was released from prison in 1981, he went back to Michigan and got a job as a graphic artist. By night, he honed his stand-up comedy act in local clubs. Soon he was touring the region.

One night in Akron, Ohio, he noticed something about the audience that was to change his act forever and start him on the road to success. He noticed that most of the men were busy eating steak, drinking beer and not paying much attention to his routine. They would eat and sit back and make grunting noises. Tim started to imitate them to get their attention. It became his famous "AR, AR, AR!" ape-like grunting sound. He had hit on a winner!

The men began to sit up and listen. He started talking about men, their tools and their marriages. Men and women alike loved the act. One night HBO taped his performance and aired it nationally. It brought him overnight fame. Soon he was getting calls from big comedy clubs in Los Angeles and all over the country. One call sent him in a direction he had never dreamed of.

Disney studios called and wanted to feature him in one of two television shows they had in mind. Amazingly, Tim turned both ideas down. Neither majored on his strengths in tool jokes. Instead, he proposed a situation comedy based on his own stand-up routine about a man who runs a tool show in Detroit with a wife and three boys. Disney liked the idea and with Tim's input, created the sitcom, *Home Improvement*. The show was so strongly shaped by Tim's influence that they even did an episode where he and his television family dealt with drugs -- to reflect his own experience.

Home Improvement skyrocketed to Number 1 in the ratings. It was in a time when most television executives were writing off traditional situation comedies. Tim proved them wrong. When he appeared on *The Tonight Show with Johnny Carson,* it was the fulfillment of a life-long dream. What made it even more special was that Tim was asked to come talk to Johnny after his routine. Most first-time comedians were given a break by coming on the show, but didn't warrant an interview. For a new comedian to be asked to sit on the sofa was a surprising honor.

Disney wanted to capitalize on Tim's popularity, so he was offered the starring role in an upcoming movie about a divorced father who reluctantly takes on the role of Santa Claus to please his son. *The Santa Clause* became a Number 1 hit.

By 1993, Tim was the star of both the top movie and top television program in the country. He was the winner of The People's Choice Male Entertainer of the Year and the author of the Number 1 book, **Don't Stand Too Close to a Naked Man** on the *New York Times'* bestseller's list.

Always a savvy negotiator, Tim's contract reflected his success. He was offered the highest sum for a lead in the history of television at that date. In 1995, he starred in Disney's *Toy Story* as the voice of Buzz Lightyear. Other live action and animation movies followed.

Tim's popularity was at the top in 1997. He was getting over $1.25 million per episode on *Home Improvement.* He started his own signature tool line with the proceed going to children's charity, modeled after Paul Newman's successful condiments business.

Then, it all almost came tumbling down when he was arrested for DUI in 1998. This was a wake-up call that he was letting his personal life slip into a dangerous area. He immediately went through a recovery program to be free from alcohol.

Shortly afterward, Disney offered him $3 million per episode. Surprisingly, Tim turned it down. He didn't want the show to run out its welcome and knew when to back away. The show went out in style with a retrospective of past highlights.

In 1999, he was awarded an honorary doctorate from his *alma mater,* Western Michigan University. That same year, he starred in *Toy Story 2* and *Galaxy Quest,* a spoof of the Star Trek phenomenon. That same year, he separated from his wife, Laura of over 15 years. Although his marriage ended, by all accounts, he remained a very devoted and caring father to his daughter, Kathryn. In 2000 and 2001, he starred in two more movies and his popularity continues to this day. *Home Improvement* is as much a hit in syndication as it was originally and probably will be for quite some time.

Tim Allen's story is one of triumph over personal demons -- a story of succeeding when you believe in yourself, a story of taking advantage of opportunities when they are placed before you. Although he started as a stand-up comedian, Tim Allen has made his mark as an author, a movie star, a philanthropist and a devoted father.

DEREK REDMOND

In 1991, Derek Redmond, Great Britain's best runner in the Men's 400 Meter event broke his own record (set in 1987) by 1/100th of a second. It was a national record that he held going into the 1992 Olympic Games in Barcelona. Derek's life goal was to win a Gold Medal in these games.

When the day came for the semi-finals in the 400 meter event, Derek knew it would be the race of his life against the world's best runners When the gun sounded, Derek got off to a great start. Then tragically, the right hamstring tore in his leg, sending him tumbling to the track surface before a packed stadium and a worldwide audience watching on television.

Paramedics rushed to assist him, as he lay writhing in pain on the ground. For most runners, the race would have ended there, but not for Derek Redmond. In agony, Derek struggled to his feet and immediately felt the pain of the torn muscle surge through his body. Then, unexpectedly, he began hopping crazily toward the finish line. As the paramedics approached him, he waved them off, grimacing in tears. The stunned crowd could not believe what they were seeing.

Then the drama took yet another twist.

A large man in a cap and t-shirt bounded out of the stands. Security guards tried to stop him, but the man flung them out of his way. He went straight for Derek. Approaching his son, Jim Redmond, put his arm around the hopping runner and said, "Son, you don't have to do this!"

"Yes, I do, Dad," Derek replied, fighting through the tears and agony.

"Then we'll finish this thing together," the father said. And that's what the two men did.

"Keep me in Lane 5!" Derek shouted, as the crowd rose to its feet. Derek's father did just that. With Derek's head buried in his father's shoulder, the two of them made it to the finish line. The audience cheered and cried as they gave them a standing ovation.

Derek didn't win an Olympic Gold Medal, but he came away with something more valuable – the knowledge that life often buries us in pain. Many times, we surrender and allow the caretakers to carry us off. We give up on our goal.

But Derek Redmond had two things working for him that day: the desire to run the complete race and a father whose love for his son surpassed any obstacle. Derek showed the world that a commitment to a goal will help you to not only finish the race, but it can inspire others to help you reach your goal. His example was so inspiring that the crowd rose to its feet an cheered. Those of us who saw it – in person or on television – will never forget the sight. It's a vivid example of the great human capacity for overcoming obstacles – with the help of those we love.

PART VII
Making Next Year Even Better

chapter 20
TAKE THIS JOB AND LOVE IT!

"Work for the fun of it, and the money will arrive some day."
-Ronnie Millsap

*T*hink you've got a bad job? Drew Carey, the comedian, once worked in Las Vegas as a waiter at Denny's. Confucius, the great Chinese philosopher once worked as a lowly grain inspector. We've all been there.

At one time or another, everybody seems to complain about their job. Either your pay isn't enough, your conditions are intolerable, your co-workers don't pull their own weight or your boss is too overbearing. MSNBC.com reported that, as of September, 2003, job satisfaction in America had dropped to the lowest point it's been since 1995. At the time of the poll, only 48.9% of American workers were satisfied with their jobs. That was almost 10% less than the 59% job satisfaction found in 1995. MSNBC found that the most dissatisfied Americans were between the ages of 45-55. Curiously enough, the most satisfied were workers over 65. In fact, they were the only group to show more people satisfied than not (54%) with their jobs overall.

What caused such a dramatic drop in job satisfaction? A weak economy? Reduced pay scales? According to the Conference Board, a New York-based research group, the top reasons were lack of promotion opportunities, fewer bonus plans and poor job training. Lynn Franco, Director of the Conference Board, said, "As technology transforms the workplace -- accelerating the pace of activities, increasing expectations and productivity demands, and blurring the lines between work and play -- workers are steadily growing more unhappy with their jobs." Other recent surveys show that worker loyalty is at an all-time low. I believe it.

I talk to many business leaders who say they feel their employees are just in it for the paycheck, without any loyalty to the organization or to the product or service the company renders to customers. Many workers tell me they are waiting for an upswing in the economy so they can look for a new job. Online job banks, like Monster.com have flourished and gained more acceptance among job seekers and company HR managers. A majority of people are discontent with their jobs. It's clear.

Me? I love what I do! Sure, there are days that I spend more time doing mundane duties that help support my speaking, but on the whole I think it's about the best job in the world. Some time, I'll tell you why I never plan to retire. Want to know my secret?

CAN'T GET NO SATISFACTION?

I can only share what works for me. In my experience, people who apply these principles spend no time at all job surfing on Monster.com. They really love what they do.

1. Learn to see the value in what you do.

What product do you produce? What service do you provide? Do you feel that it is something that adds value to others lives? Do you feel that people are better off with your goods and services? Do you have a deep-seated conviction that people actually need or will benefit from what you produce? Often we lose sight of our service or product's value during the regular work-a-day world on the job.

While sitting in the doctor's office the other today, I heard a man talking to a woman about what he does. He rebuilds brake pads on eighteen-wheel trucks. He said his shop is the best in the business and that trucking companies rely on him to keep their drivers and products safe. He said this with a pride in his voice that spoke of his feeling of uniqueness.

"No one else does what I do as well as I do it," he told her, with confidence.

Wow! I'd hate doing what he does for a living, but he not only likes it, he considers himself the best. Sure, he may only be the best in his own eyes, but isn't that what is most important?

Shouldn't we all feel we're the best at what we do? I'm sure the truck drivers who know him are appreciative, but that's just icing on the cake for him.

I remember meeting with the National W.I.F.E. (Women Involved in Farm Economics) Convention last year. Farmers have taken a beating in the past 40 years, but these men and women were proud that they grew produce and cattle better than anyone else in the world. There will always be a call for American farmers' products, because farming is one of the things Americans do best.

2. **Find what you like to do.**

About ten years ago, a friend gave me this advice: "Jim, spend the first part of your life finding what you like to do. Then in the second half, get people to pay you to do it!"

What do you like so much that you would do it, even if nobody paid you to do it?

Finding out it the first step!

Remember what Curly, Jack Palance's crusty character in "City Slickers" said, "The meaning of life is just one thing. Get that right and nothing else matters..."

Finding the thing you enjoy, the thing you'd like to do better than anyone else is just like finding the meaning of life. Maybe it's not the grand, ultimate meaning. But it's your meaning. And that's all you need to get started.

What is your one thing? When you find it, you'll realize that not everybody likes doing it as much as you. Not everybody can be as good at it as you can be, either. That's why it's so important to find your thing and make it your own. You're the best one to do it!

Every week, I get up in front of large crowds of people to speak, train or entertain. I like it, but not everybody would. In fact, when people list their biggest fear, getting up in front of a large audience, is usually No. 1. It's amazing to me that they fear speaking more than falling – which is my biggest fear! They fear it more than spiders and snakes, which come in very high on most people's lists.

Yet, for me, speaking is like heaven! There's nothing I'd rather do for a living. And I took my friend's good advice. I spent the first half of my life finding what I like to do. Now, in the second half, I'm making a living at it.

I come from a family of educators. My father, my mother, my aunt and my grandmother were all teachers or school administrators. They loved teaching. Sure, they had headaches on the job -- terrible ones -- but they valued what they did in young people's lives. They had a natural respect for knowledge and commitment that more education would make you a better person. This came out in the way each taught their students. My brother-in-law switched careers at about age 50 to teach high school and he loves it. He'd always enjoyed instructing. Now he gets paid to do it.

What would you do if there were no pay involved?

On those days when the pay isn't enough to help you overcome your problems, your love of what you do will be there to get you through it, which brings us to the next point.

3. **Have a positive, healthy attitude about problems on the job.**

Everyone's job is fraught with difficulties. Problems occur all the time. It's how you view them that makes the difference. Either they are solvable or they are a continuing string of setbacks. Problems can be opportunities for you to learn from. Your perspective makes the difference.

I once heard a former COO tell a group that problems aren't opportunities. He managed a trucking firm and said that when he had a truck broken down on the side of the road that was nothing but a problem. Sometimes, to find opportunities inside of problems, you have to know how to look.

Even when everything goes wrong, there's an opportunity. If you're the COO and one of your trucks breaks down on the side of the road, it's a problem. No question. It's also an opportunity to show that trucker that you'll be there to rescue him and get him going again. It's an opportunity to show other employees how you will support a lone employee stranded on the highway. Breakdowns are inevitable. But if this COO had turned every breakdown into an opportunity to increase employee loyalty by showing how he would always be there to rescue and support them, he may end up being grateful for those breakdowns in the long run!

As I've mentioned before, Norman Vincent Peale said, "Every problem has in it the seeds of its own solution. If you don't have any problems, you don't get any seeds." Did you know that every miracle in the Bible began with a problem, If you have a problem, you're a candidate for a miracle. If you don't have a problem, then you don't get a miracle. It's up to you whether you see yourself as a candidate for a miracle or not. If you don't look, you don't see the opportunity inside the problem and you don't become a candidate for a miracle. What a different a positive, healthy attitude makes!

4. **Learn to beat your "blahs."**

Everyone gets the blahs, but many get them every week on schedule. Mondays are traditionally the worst day of everyone's work week and with some good reasons.

Did you know that you are more likely to drop dead from a heart attack on a Monday than any other day of the week? One great stock market crash occurred on Monday, October 19, 1987. The Dow Jones Industrial average slipped over 508 points on that day. On other notable Mondays in history: The Titanic sank. The atomic bomb was dropped on Hiroshima. Jesse James was shot and killed. And Ford Motor Company introduced an exciting new car proposal, called the Edsel on, you guessed it, a Monday.

Most people don't need a Monday to start pitying themselves, though. They are practitioners of the wrong thinking and the wrong pity.

Eugene H. Peterson says, "Pity is one of the noblest emotions available to human beings; self-pity is possibly the most ignoble." He goes on to say, "Pity is adrenaline for acts of mercy; self-pity is a narcotic that leaves its addicts wasted and derelict."

To avoid self-pity over your job, ask yourself these questions: What are you doing to liven up your job? How can you see something new each day? How can you instill challenge and anticipation into a mundane task? Many people when suffering setbacks ask the question, "Why?" They never make real progress in their lives, because they never stop looking back and asking why. They can't proceed until they move beyond that question.

5. **Dress for success.**

Appearance plays a major role in our attitudes about work. It often reflects an inner happiness or dissatisfaction. Do you dress for success?

Drab people usually dress accordingly. Color has an enormous impact on our emotions. Workspace color as well influences our attitudes. To raise your excitement level, yellow and red are good. Blues and greens tend to have a calming effect on us.

Learn to personalize your appearance and work area, where possible. Find ways to lift your spirits with a splash of color! Even if it's changing the screen saver or desktop image on your computer regularly, do something to liven your emotions.

Eric Hoffer says, "When people are bored, it is primarily with their own selves that they are bored."

Verbal "appearance" says a lot, too. Change your voice mail frequently to something better. How you present yourself makes a lasting impression on people.

6. **Reward yourself for a good day's work.**

This is a good exercise to start learning how to set goals. Set personal goals. Set work-related personal goals. Set goals each day and week. Make them substantial, but attainable. Practice setting small ones at first. When you achieve them give yourself a "bonus." Then progressively each week raise the bar.

Set goals that stretch you. Start dreaming BIG. Then, be sure to reward yourself each time you are successful. Make it something worthwhile to you. You are a better authority on what reward gets you motivated than anyone else. What activities do you enjoy most? Some people treat themselves to a nice dinner, a round of golf, a weekend trip or a shopping spree. Go ahead and spoil yourself. You've earned it and you deserve it.

7. **Invest in others.**

Dr. Georgia Witkin, a noted psychologist, says that it is almost impossible to be bogged down with negative feelings when you are busy helping someone else. Remember the first step in loving your job? Find value in what you produce for others. Find value in your job by reaching out to co-workers. Often you'll probably find they are suffering from the same feelings that have kept you down. Even in suffering, there's strength in numbers.

I have a change presentation that includes having people change their appearance several times in a few minutes ("Managing Change," see Keynote Topics ,or Articles on Change at www.jimmathis.com). It's fun and funny to watch. Every time I lead a group in this exercise, though, participants look at themselves for ideas of things to change, not at others in the room going through the same changes. It surprises them when I tell them at the end that there were at least 25 things they could have changed by just looking around at everyone else in the room. But they always look down at themselves first and say they can't think of any changes to make. Hold your head up! Look around to see who else is going through the same emotions you are. Help each other out.

8. **If you can't be satisfied with what you do, find what you want to do -- and do it.**

Launch out! If you don't like what you're doing now, what have you got to lose?

Most businesses fail in the first three years because of a lack of confidence and commitment on the part of the entrepreneur. They don't realize that it takes commitment to that one thing they like doing over everything else.

Sure, it may be rough at first. Everything worth having is worth sacrifice. Find what you like to do and determine to do it no matter what it takes.

Radio talk show host Dave Ramsey says you can do it in 48 days. Just think, you could be a month-and-a-half away from a new, exciting and more beneficial career. Society will be a better place for it -- you'll be better, too.

Chapter 21

HOW TO BE FINANCIALLY HAPPY
9.5 IDEAS YOU CAN IMPLEMENT NOW!

"If you see yourself as prosperous, you will be.
If you see yourself as continually hard up, that is exactly what you will be."
-Robert Collier

I am a fan of old television shows. I love the classics from the 60's and 70's: *I Love Lucy, Happy Days, The Dick Van Dyke Show* and my all-time favorite, *The Andy Griffith Show.*

If you've seen these shows too, did you ever notice how happy all of these characters are? The writers consistently told stories about people who didn't have much money, but were happy with life in general.

In this genre, there was only one show about an American family with a lot of money, but even then the money wasn't said to be the source of their happiness. In fact, the Clampetts were simple folk who would have been just as happy without their fortune. I'm referring of course to the show, *The Beverly Hillbillies.* The writers were telling a parable about life. Week after week, the most contented people on the show were the ones who didn't spend too much or hoard what they had and the Clampetts themselves were completely unchanged by the money that had come their way.

Frederich Koenig said, "We tend to forget that happiness doesn't come as a result of getting something we don't have, but rather of recognizing and appreciating what we do have."

There's a lesson to be learned from being content with what you have. What does it take to become financially happy? What are steps you can take to make your bottom-line more secure?

Here are 10 ideas to get the new year off on the right foot. It's NOT a plan to make more money. It is 10 steps to help you be happy with what you have and to keep more of it.

1. **Pay as you go.**

Pay your bills when they come in. Most people put off paying their bills either until they are due or until a certain a period of time. This misleads them in to thinking they have more money than they do.

G. Randolph said, "Pay as you go is the philosopher's stone." Pay as you go and you will have a realistic viewpoint as to what you have in your bank account. Anticipate the bills coming in by keeping the money in your checking account to cover them, then pay them the day they arrive.

Trust me, you'll know what you have and be happier about it. Roy Goodman said, "Remember that happiness is a way of travel, not a destination."

2. **Minimize your credit card debt.**

According to the Credit Counseling Center in Dallas, Texas, the average American household has $12,000 in credit card debt! That figure is double what it was ten years ago. Dr. Joyce Brothers once wrote, "Credit buying is much like being drunk. The buzz happens immediately and it gives you a lift. The hangover comes the day after."

I listen to media financial advisers like Clark Howard and Dave Ramsey and Suze Orman. Most people who call in to their nationally syndicated radio and television shows are in credit card debt up past their eyeballs. People will call in who are $20,000 in debt from credit cards. Don't fool yourself into thinking you'll have more money later. Don't rely on your credit cards to tide you over till then. The day may never come.

By the way, did you know that you can call some credit card companies and request a lower finance rate on your card. You won't know if yours does until you try.

3. **Save 5% of your income.**

Most people have no savings plan and if their company wasn't putting money into their retirement, they wouldn't have any money there either.

We like to spend money the moment we get it and spend it when we don't even have it. Start putting just 5% into a savings account and leave it alone!

It's like the old adage of the ant and the grasshopper. The ant saved for the winter while the grasshopper played and spent all he had. When winter came, the ant was ready. If we have another recession or an emergency arises in your life (your own personal winter), how ready will you be?

4. **Communicate with your spouse and family about finances.**

In another film, *Raising Arizona,* two escaped convicts come to Hi and Ed's home and find them squabbling. John Goodman, who plays one of the escaped cons, says, "This is about finances, isn't it, Hi?" He's raising the point that most family disagreements are over finances and poor communication.

Learn to communicate positively about spending, budgets and cash flow in your home. Who is spending what , where and when? Who is responsible for balancing the checkbook? Are you keeping to the family/household budget? Ask now or you will regret it later.

5. **Work toward your goals.**

Do you have personal goals? Did you know that less than 33% of people today even have goals? Most of them haven't written them down anywhere.

Learn to set goals for yourself, your family and your organization, then work toward them. Find small ways to reward yourself at each step toward your goal.

Just by writing down and reviewing them once a month you will be ahead of most of the population. Write them down everywhere. In your calendar, your day timer, your brief case, the wall of your office, in your car and even on your cell phone memo text pad.

Surveys have show that we need to be reminded of our goals about once every 26-30 days.

6. **Spend responsibly.**

Don't be consumed with a desire for more and learn to live within your means. Vernon Howard once said, "You have succeeded in life when all you really want is only what you really need."

One way to keep your spending down is to negotiate lower prices for items you need. Almost everything is negotiable, including mortgage rates -- we just fail to negotiate.

Most people assume that the list price on an item is non-negotiable. We negotiate for cars and houses. I negotiate for everything: cell phone service, insurance coverage, home theater equipment and many other items. I save money and always leave with a win-win situation.

Why would you want to buy something if you knew you could get it for 10%-50% cheaper by shopping around or by discussing the price a little? Give it a try. You may be surprised by the results.

Don't buy anything you know you don't have to have. Don't buy when the price is low, but you don't have the money to cover the purchase. It'll be low again, and sooner than you think.

7. **Keep up with your cash.**

Save receipts. Know where your money is and how much you have.

Don't fear your cash, respect it. We work hard to get money then we act spend like it took nothing to obtain it. Don't overfill your wallet. Put in just enough to get by on and live on that.

Oliver Goldsmith said, "If frugality were established in the state, and if our expenses were laid out to meet needs rather than superfluities of life, there might be fewer wants, and even fewer pleasures, but infinitely more happiness."

Stop going to the ATM machine or getting extra cash back at the store. Live on a weekly budget, and when it runs out, you're out. Now I know you're saying that emergencies will come up (see the step on saving 5%) or that you can't live once the money runs out. You will be surprised how little you'll spend on useless things when you have to live on a little.

8. Get organized.

Start a filing system for bills, receipts, coupons, savings accounts, and investments. People heavily in debt usually can't tell you where the money is or went. If that's you, don't be afraid to ask for help. Often you can get it free or for a one-time fee.

Accountants would rather see you organized than have you bring in a pile of papers and dump them on their desk. Our accountant told us one time that if we had not gotten a return on our taxes, we would have spent the excess money and not known where it had gone. He was probably right. Here's a question for you: Do you know where every penny went from your tax rebate this past year? Most people will answer "No." If you know, you are ahead of them already.

9. Give money away.

That's right, give money away. The wealthiest people usually are the best (not biggest, mind you) givers. Why? They've learned that you get by giving. You get satisfaction, you get fulfillment, you get tax breaks and you get the peace that you are helping others.

Give to the United Way, the Red Cross, the church, AmeriCares or some other charity that helps others and you believe in. There is a line in the song, *Life's a Dance*, that says. "The longer I live the more I believe, you have to give if you want to receive."

I heard a tape a month ago that said: "Imagine you are God and you want to bless someone. Would you give prosperity to someone who hoards everything and doesn't share or would you give it to the person who shares and makes the world a better place?" Maybe you don't have much because you don't give much. John Fountain said, "Happy were men if they but understood there is no safety but in doing good."

9.5.   START NOW!

Just do it. Don't put these steps off until a more opportune time. There won't ever be one. Decide today, right now, that you will implement all of these ideas. Decide to keep more of your money by keeping track of it, by not spending it foolishly, by not accumulating more debt than what you have and by giving some of it away.

Nothing you've read here is new. I didn't originate any of the 10 steps. This is advice you can get anywhere -- *Fortune* or *Money* magazines, Clark Howard, Dave Ramsey or Suze Orman -- but most people don't take the time to act on it.

Here's a shocker, 98% of the people reading this will not act on it in the next 24 hours. You can beat them all by starting now. What are you waiting for?

chapter 22

BACKWARDS PLANNING:
6 SIMPLE RULES FOR SCHEDULING NEXT YEAR

"The trouble with many plans
is that they are based on the way things are now.
To be successful, your personal plan must
focus on what you want, not what you have."
-Nido Qubein

Recently, while I was conducting a time management training seminar at the end of the year, I was amazed to find out how many managers still had no clue about how to plan their schedule or set their goals for the coming year.

I am surprised anything gets done in business with so many leaders who can't make proper plans. There is an old adage that says: "He who fails to plan, plans to fail."

Looking back at my own career in business, I realize that most managers I worked for planned their goals and schedules to fail. They set out with a misguided agenda, so, of course, they spent the next year in damage control. Then when the next planning time came, they were left wondering what went wrong.

It's said that "the more you do of what you're doing, the more you'll get of what you've got." Tired of getting the same results year and year out? It is time to start planning for success. It is time to try something different.

Here are 6 Simple Rules to guide you in planning ahead for success in the year ahead.

1. **RESULTS – Try planning backwards.**
Start with the results in mind. Most people plan around their schedule in an effort to "fill up the calendar." If your goal is to stay busy, this is a great idea. But if your goal is to accomplish something like -- oh, I don't know -- improve your career, meet new financial markers, or make real strides in any area at all, this is the dumbest way to start out. Really, what are you trying to accomplish this year? Move the sand pile to the left, then move it back to the right?

Smart planners begin with the results they want to achieve. They ruthlessly eliminate everything that doesn't support this goal. They never hesitate to say, "No, that's not what we are about." Great leaders stay focused on the main thing they and never deter from it.

What do you want to see occur next year? Where do you want to be? Set that as your planning goal and make everything else fall in to place around it. Guard this and don't let any other activity or program get in the way.

2. ACTIVITIES – Plan the activities that will accomplish your goal(s).

Don't schedule them yet. Just sit down and determine what it will take to get to the destination you have set.

Some activities may be impossible to pull off, but this will give you a good idea of what you need to be doing and how you need to distribute resources to get things done. Planning activities will help you determine the Big Three questions that need to be answered in planning guidelines:

1. What do you *think* you are doing?
2. What *should* you be doing?
3. What are you *actually* doing?

Examining all three perspectives will give you valuable insight into your job and time problems.

Activities that don't meet these criteria or don't support the mission of your company, corporation or mission should be eliminated, no matter how sacred they are.

How many exercises do you do for no other reason than, we've always done them? Read *Sacred Cows Make Great Burgers*. It's an excellent book about getting things done.

Yes, it is risky to ask "Why?" but you've got to take a few risks to venture into new territory. Have some fun. Go around and ask people how certain historical practices originated and why they continue to schedule them every year. You'll be surprised at how many people are clueless, but continue to perform them like mindless sheep.

3. PRIORITIES – Get consensus

This step will happen almost automatically. Once you begin to re-evaluate your priorities and find out what you need to be about in the year ahead, you'll be surprised to find how easy it is to eliminate useless activities that don't accomplish your mission or goals.

Determining your goals and activities will help you establish clear priorities for the time period you are planning. It will help you enforce the "If it doesn't support or goals, we're not doing it" rule.

Use the Paretto Principle to establish your priorities: "Eighty percent of our activities produce 20 percent of the results, while only 20 percent of our activities produce 80 percent of the results." Vilifredo Paretto was a 19th Century Italian economist who established a rule for economics that works in almost every realm of planning.

It is simple: List your top ten priorities in order, then circle the top two. Concentrate planning on those two and the other eight will take care of themselves. More organizations waste time on useless trivial activities that produce almost no results. The wisdom of life consists of eliminating the non-essentials.

4. **TIME ESTIMATES – Find out how long it will take.**

How much time will each activity require to get you closer to your annual goals? The key to successful planning is to plan both work and time. Start to determine what will take big blocks of time, what will be required to get it done and where will you find the resources needed to accomplish each task.

Next, look at the smaller blocks of time and find out how they can be batched together to eliminate waste in funding and time. Where are the wasted time slots? How can they be reduced or wiped away completely?

Determine what time of the year is the peak performance time to get each task accomplished. Where are the slow periods annually that you can get more "behind the scenes" work done? When is your "showtime," when visible tasks are best accomplished? Remember these are only estimates but they will give you a good idea as to when you need to be concentrating on the right tasks at the right time.

5. **SCHEDULING – Scheduled things tend to happen on time.**

Now look at your actual calendar. Things that are not scheduled may never happen. As I said earlier, most managers tend to schedule first in an effort to fill the calendar and eliminate gaps. Knowing what you are about, why you are about it, and how long it will take will be the greatest ally you have in putting things on in ink.

Use these guidelines for scheduling:

> Keep flexibility in time.
> Start early on major efforts.
> Put the big blocks first.
> Put smaller jobs/activities second.
> Group items together that are similar in nature.

Scheduling along these lines will do more to eliminate wasted time in your calendar. It will allow for the time estimates to become realities and your people to know what they are doing, why they are doing it and how it fits into your overall mission/goals.

6. FLEXIBILITY – Allow time for error and the uncertainty.

This can only be done if you have set out to allow the proper amount of time for big projects. No one can predict the future (although we seem to have an abundance of philosophers, pundits and fanatics who attempt to do it every day).

Last year, a well-known television economist spent the first two months of his new program telling everyone not to buy home improvement company stocks (Lowe's, Home Depot, etc.), then was forced to retract every prediction when they soared following the devastating hurricanes in the Gulf Coast areas.

One good rule: Don't take advice from anyone who isn't personally invested in the suggestions they are giving. You probably have example in your own life of people who said to do one thing only to change when things weren't as certain as they assured you. Don't get stuck paying the bill for their mistakes.

Planning flexibility allows you to adjust your schedule as needed. It allows you to drop back and re-evaluate your intentions and redistribute resources and personnel in key areas as are required. Be flexible about your schedule, but not about your results or goals. Times change and although you can't predict the future, the great leaders are able to see through the present times and prepare for both good and bad events. Those with the best outlook on life are always expecting the best, but prepared for the worst, just in case. To deny that problems will arise is foolishness.

Our ability to control our time is directly related to our attitude toward controlling our environment. If you follow these guidelines, you will be in control of your schedule. You will be able to determine what to do and when to do it based on a simple rule: What results do I want? Mary Kay Ash said, "If you think you can, you can. If you think you can't, you are right."

A year from today, evaluate the tasks you have accomplished. How well did you meet your goals? How long did it take to get in step with the master plan and find ways to cut wasted time and reallocate resources? How prepared were you for unforeseen events in the market and society? How much more can you accomplish next year? Try "Backwards Planning" and see how everything fits better into place.

Chapter 23

9 STEPS FOR MAKING THIS YOUR BEST YEAR EVER!

"Always bear in mind that your own resolution
to succeed is more important than any one thing."
-Abraham Lincoln

1. **Act like the person you wish to become.**

Start thinking positively by acting positively. Don't wait until you feel like taking action, take it!

Form the habit of *seizing the moment* right now.

Model this attitude for those around you. Watch their reaction and see how it spreads among your friends and loved ones. Remember, people are watching you. You have a ready opportunity to serve as a positive role model in your life on almost a daily basis.

2. **Cultivate a consistent positive attitude.**

Begin thinking positively about situations that confront you. Your health will improve.

If you want a full garden, you have to plow, plant, water, trim and weed frequently throughout the year. If you want a successful life, it won't happen over night. It, too, takes time and work. If you don't pay attention to your crop, weeds will infect it and you'll have a life of negative attitudes. Focus on the positive and don't feed the weeds.

3. **Look for the best in everyone.**

Have you ever noticed that when you buy a new car, you suddenly notice others of that same model and year on the road? They didn't just appear. They were there all along. You just started noticing them. In the same way, train yourself to look for the best in everyone around you. When you consistently look for the best in others, their food traits will have a positive affect on your life and leadership.

4. **Look for the best in new ideas.**

Have you ever seen a good idea and said, "I wish I'd thought of that"? I know I have. The truth is, the process of coming up with good ideas is more attitude than aptitude. An open-minded, creative person looks for ideas anywhere he can.

Failure often causes people to go out and try it another way. Thomas Edison, one of history's greatest inventors, discovered some of his best inventions after other ideas went wrong and he was forced to find another use for them. Ivory soap and Noxzema were both created out of failed attempts to find something else. If you keep an open mind and explore every idea presented to you, those in your sphere of influence will follow your example. The new ideas you discover together will contribute to your mutual success.

5. **Decide not to quit.**

Most leaders fail because they give up too easily. When he was a boy, Lance Armstrong's mother told him, "Pain is temporary. Quitting is forever." He never forgot it. It has helped him go on to be one of the most successful athletes in history.

Are you putting everything you have into your job? If you aren't, maybe that's why your workers aren't. If they feel you've given up on a project or another worker, the attitude spreads and they adopt it as a lifestyle.

6. **Don't be afraid to take risks.**

Any broker will tell you that the stocks that produce the most reward are the riskiest ones. Orchard owners will tell you that the best fruit is always way out on the limb.

Don't be afraid to stretch your comfort zone. Push yourself and you will be amazed at how far you will go and grow!

7. **Serve others.**

The success of the National Speaker's Association is grounded in a commitment begun by its founder, Cavett Robert. Robert spent his life helping others to be their best. He founded the NSA on the principle of enlarging the pie, rather than seeing how it could be cut up. Volunteer your time in local causes that lift others up.

Model servanthood to those who look up to you. Think about the stores, restaurants and businesses you like to do business with. You'll find that they serve you effectively and continually make you feel important. Base your organization on this principle and see the difference it will make in your customers.

8. **Keep your sights set on your goal.**

In the ancient world, farmers often used a tree, a stone or another stationary land   mark to guide them in plowing their fields. It was important for a farmer to keep his eyes on that marker to plow a straight furrow. Life is like that.
Don't let the little things take your eyes off of the goals you have set for yourself. Make sure to keep the main thing, the main thing.

We all need to be reminded of our goals at least every 30 days. Find ways to remind yourself and guarantee you stay on track. At the end of the year, when you look back to see how much you've accomplished, you'll be glad you kept your eyes on the goal.

9. **Use time wisely.**

One of my friends has a successful sales training business. He likes to say that most sales aren't closed because time is wasted. Even his website says, "Why are you sitting there reading this page when you could be out selling something?"

Procrastination kills not only time, but enthusiasm and drive as well. It will be great year if you use all of it judiciously. Why not start right now?!

PROFILES

WALT DISNEY

The creator of Mickey Mouse, founder of Disneyland, Walt Disney World Theme Parks and the Walt Disney Corporate empire was born on December 5, 1901 in Chicago. His father, Elias Disney, was an Irish-Canadian. His mother was of German-American descent. Walt was one of five children -- four boys and a girl. He was raised on a farm near Marceline, Missouri.

Walt became interested in drawing at an early age. He sold his first sketches to neighbors when he was only seven years old. The family moved several times in his life: to Kansas City, Missouri and back to Chicago. During his high school days in Chicago, Disney divided his interest between drawing, photography and working on the school paper. At night, he attended the Academy of Fine Arts to perfect his talent.

When America entered the First World War, Walt attempted to enlist in the military to serve his country, but he was rejected because he was only 16. So he joined the Red Cross and was sent overseas, where he spent a year driving an ambulance. On the outside, his ambulance was covered from one end to the other with drawings and cartoons, instead of camouflage.

After the war, Walt returned to Kansas City, where he began his career as an advertising cartoonist. Here, in 1920, he created and marketed his first original, animated cartoons and later perfected a new method for combining live action and animation.

While Walt was creating *The Alice Comedies*, about a real girl and her adventures in an animated world, he ran out of money and his company went bankrupt. Instead of quitting, Walt packed his suitcase and with his unfinished print of *The Alice Comedies* in hand, headed for Hollywood to start a new business at the age of twenty-one.

The early flop of *The Alice Comedies* didn't discourage Walt, but it gave him a respect for failure. He would risk everything three or four times in his life to succeed.

Walt's brother, Roy Disney, was already in California and offered him both encouragement and financial backing. The two brothers borrowed an additional $500, and set up shop in their uncle's garage. Soon, they received an order from New York for the first *Alice in Cartoonland (The Alice Comedies)* short feature and expanded their production operation in the rear of a real estate office. It was Walt's enthusiasm and faith in himself and others that led him on the road to success. Hollywood would never be the same as a result of his perseverance.

On July 13, 1925, Walt married one of his first employees, Lillian Bounds, in Lewiston, Idaho. They would be blessed with two daughters, Diane and Sharon. Three years after Walt and Lilly wed, Walt created a new animated character who would prove to be his breakthrough, Mickey Mouse. (It is a well-known fact that Walt had a fear of mice.)

Mickey made his screen debut in *Steamboat Willie*, the world's first synchronized sound cartoon, which premiered at the Colony Theater in New York on November 18, 1928. Walt himself provided Mickey's original voice. Walt continually worked to perfect his animation techniques. Every new cartoon showed improvement over the previous ones. He wisely held the patent for Technicolor for two years, allowing him to make the only color cartoons.

In 1932, the production entitled *Flowers and Trees* won Walt the first of his studio's Academy Awards. In 1937 he released *Snow White and the Seven Dwarfs*, the first full-length animated musical feature, which premiered in Los Angeles. He literally acted out the film in the office of a financial backer to win his approval. During the next five years, Walt Disney Studios completed other full-length animated classics such as *Pinocchio*, *Fantasia*, *Dumbo*, and *Bambi*.

His success brought him great fame and fortune. But a painful episode occurred, just as things were taking off in his life. With their new success, he and Roy had bought their parents a home close to their Burbank studios. Less than a month later, his mother died of asphyxiation, caused by a faulty furnace in the new home. Blaming himself, Walt carried the guilt of this tragedy for the rest of his life.

During World War II , the Disney studios and employees were engaged in special projects for the U.S. Government, some of which are still shown throughout the world today. He was still able to devote time to the production of comedy short subjects to boost civilian and military morale. This was the start of the "Golden Age" for Walt Disney.

In a groundbreaking move, Walt's 1945 film, *The Three Caballeros*, combined live action with the cartoon animation. It was a process that he used in other features such as *Song of the South* and the award-winning *Mary Poppins*. More than 100 features were produced by his studio. Later Disney expanded into live-action features, like *Treasure Island* (1951), and then into television – with a family variety program *The Wonderful World of Disney*, which was a hit from 1954-83. During Disney's life, his studios won 48 Academy Awards.

Walt had a vision of creating entertainment that would allow families to enjoy time together. In 1955, he opened a theme park, Disneyland, in Anaheim, California. It was an immediate hit and became the public flagship of the Disney empire. Other larger Disney theme parks followed in Florida, Tokyo and France. The Florida operation also embodied his dream of the future in EPCOT (Experimental Prototype Community of Tomorrow).

Walttook a deep interest in the establishment of California Institute of the Arts. Of Cal Arts, Walt once said, "It's the principal thing I hope to leave when I move on to greener pastures. If I can help provide a place to develop the talent of the future, I think I will have accomplished something."

After smoking cigarettes for much of his life, Walt succumbed to lung cancer at the age of 65 in 1966. He left a mountain of work and accomplishments that are unparalleled. With 64 Academy Award nominations, Walt Disney still holds the record for career Academy Award nominations to this day.

His optimism and visions, came from the fond memories of bygone days. His success was founded on these hopes for the future and an undying persistence in making his dreams come true. It was his lifelong mission to make life more enjoyable, and fun. He is remembered around the world as a creative genius who bridged the past to the future.

LANCE ARMSTRONG

Born in 1971 in Dallas, Texas, Lance Armstrong has become a worldwide emblem of comebacks. In 1991, Lance won the U.S. amateur cycling championship and turned professional the following year. Lance quickly rose from amateur status to world championships, capturing 10 titles in 1993 alone. He won the prestigious Tour DuPont twice in the mid-nineties. He then competed for the U.S. Olympic team in 1992 and 1996. It seemed that nothing could stop him.

What happened next is well-known. At 25 in October 1996, Lance was diagnosed with testicular cancer and given a 50% chance of survival. In most cases, a diagnosis like this would end a person's career. But Lance Armstrong was not a quitter.

It was discovered that the cancer was widespread and he had a choice of giving up or undergoing risky surgery and chemotherapy. When they realized the cancer had spread to his brain and lungs, the doctors doubted he would live, let alone recover and then dominate the sport's most grueling event. But they didn't know Lance.

When Lance told the world about his illness, he was a world cycling champion. His popularity among bicycling enthusiasts was growing in Europe, but fewer Americans outside the fast-paced cycling world, had more than a hint of an idea who this thin young man on their television screens was -- or what he was up against.

"I'd never been sick before," said Armstrong. "I'd never had a broken bone in my body. I think the only other time I had been in the hospital was when I was born. But then I got cancer and all that changed."

Even today, Lance has a Texan's blunt brand of honesty, owning up to his fears and his shortcomings -- something very few athletes (much less Texans) ever do. For example, he says that in his "other life" before cancer, he never really believed he could win cycling's premier race, the three-week, 3000-plus mile Tour de France.

"I was a one-day rider," he said. "My teammates wanted me to win the Tour, but to be honest with you, in my mind, I didn't believe I could do it. I told them I would win, because that's what they wanted to hear. But I never believed it."

The world was shocked when he came back from his bout with testicular cancer to win the Tour de France in 1999, but it didn't end there. In 2002, Lance was named "Sportsman of the Year" by *Sports Illustrated*, after winning his fourth straight TdF. Most recently, in July, 2005, he won a record seventh straight Tour de France. People began worrying about his winning time of only 75 seconds ahead of his closest competitor in 2003, but Lance Armstrong has come to be synonymous with triumph. He won again.

Lance sums up his journey by saying,

"I learned what it means to ride in the Tour de France. It's not about the bike. It's a metaphor for life, not only the longest race in the world but also the most exalting and heartbreaking and potentially tragic. It poses every conceivable element to the rider and more. During our lives we're faced with so many elements as well, we experience so many setbacks, and fight such a hand-to-hand battle with failure, head down in the rain, just trying to stay upright and have a little hope. The Tour isn't just a bike race, it tests you mentally, physically, and even morally."

Lance's story is a comeback story, when he tells it, he seems calmly grateful. Even while he was recovering, he created the Texas-based Lance Armstrong Foundation, which provides funding and support to cancer patients and survivors.

Lance put endurance cycling on the American map like no one before him. He has become associated with it as much as Michael Jordan with professional basketball, Tiger Woods with professional golf, and Muhammad Ali with professional boxing. But even more, he is a testimony to never giving up when the odds are stacked against you.

"Cancer taught me a plan for more purposeful living, and that in turn taught me how to train and to win more purposefully. It taught me that pain has a reason, and that sometimes the experience of losing things--whether health or a car or an old sense of self--has its own value in the scheme of life. Pain and loss are great enhancers... No one automatically gives you respect just because you show up. You have to earn it." It's a life lesson for us all.